THE APOSTOLIC MI

The Apostolic Ministry

ULF EKMAN

WORD OF LIFE PUBLISHING
SWEDEN

KINGSWAY PUBLICATIONS
EASTBOURNE

ISBN 0 85476 637 5

Designed and produced by
Bookprint Creative Services
P.O. Box 827, BN21 3YJ, England for
KINGSWAY PUBLICATIONS LTD
Lottbridge Drove, Eastbourne, E. Sussex BN23 6NT.
Printed in Great Britain.

Contents

Ministry gifts are tools in the hands of the Holy Spirit that build up the body of Christ to fulfil its destiny and affect the world.

The apostolic ministry has been mentioned least and mystified most. If not denied, then it has often been defined improperly or shallowly.

Rather than provide a thorough analysis of the apostolic ministry, I want to provide a basic explanation that will clarify much of the confusion surrounding this area. Above all, I hope that this book will outline a ministry which has inspired Christians throughout the ages and which many believe still exists today. If it does, what role will it play in the Last Days?

There are many wonderful people in the Lord's service today, whose labours prompt us to recall those of the apostles in the New Testament. They are often different in style, but they set a trail, break ground and lay the foundation for strong, lasting works. They are often misunderstood, persecuted and despised, but they are loved by the Lord. I dedicate this book to them.

This book is the result of the 1991 autumn seminar at Word of Life Church, Uppsala, Sweden.

Ulf Ekman

Foreword

In recent years there have been a number of mistaken and unbiblical interpretations of the apostolic ministry. This book by Ulf Ekman needs to be read widely throughout the church, because it describes the apostolic ministry from a truly biblical perspective as a foundation ministry for the building up and equipping of God's people. As with all God-given ministry it has to centre on anointing rather than function. The function of the apostle comes out of his calling and anointing.

Ulf Ekman lays the biblical foundation for the apostolic ministry in a coherent and refreshing way. And he makes clear the specific function the ministry is to have in the body of Christ.

The apostle has a heart and vision for the whole church. He seeks to see it function in faith and in breaking new ground, but is concerned that it has stability and that what is built truly glorifies the Lord. Above all, he is concerned to see that the church fulfils its call and task to reach the *world* with the gospel. He has world vision.

Ulf emphasises the key role the apostle has to play in developing spiritual ministry and in raising up and releasing others in leadership.

There has to be a distinctiveness about the apostolic call, that God uses an apostle in ways that differ from the other ministries.

This book is written with authority because this distinctiveness is clearly seen in Ulf's own ministry.

The planting of a church does not make a person an apostle, nor the claim to oversee a number of congregations. The way in which Ulf Ekman emphasises the character of the apostle is welcome. He builds one biblical truth upon another, and so gives a true account of apostolic ministry—how it develops in the New Testament and how it is to develop now.

It is important for every Christian in every congregation to understand the importance of the apostolic anointing and to be part of the apostolic vision for God's purposes for the whole church in reaching the world with the love and power of Jesus Christ.

I pray that this book will not only increase your understanding of the apostolic function, but will show you how you can benefit from being part of such apostolic vision. For the whole church is to be truly apostolic.

Colin Urquhart

1

Aspects and Origin of the Ministry Gifts

It was he who gave some to be apostles, some to be prophets, some to be evangelists, and some to be pastors and teachers, to prepare God's people for works of service, so that the body of Christ may be built up until we all reach unity in the faith and in the knowledge of the Son of God and become mature, attaining to the whole measure of the fullness of Christ. Then we will no longer be infants, tossed back and forth by the waves, and blown here and there by every wind of teaching and by the cunning and craftiness of men in their deceitful scheming. Instead, speaking the truth in love, we will in all things grow up into him who is the Head, that is, Christ. From him the whole body, joined and held together by every supporting ligament, grows and builds itself up in love, as each part does its work (Eph 4:11–16).

The ministry gifts are mentioned throughout the Bible. This book will deal with all of them, but focus particularly on the apostle. No area of ministry has been so well documented, so well developed in the New Testament as the ministry of the apostle. Yet the apostolic ministry has often been misunderstood and poorly developed, resulting in so many variations that some have come to fear it. Sadly, we have often neglected it, causing great damage to the body of Christ. If the ministry of the apostle doesn't function properly, then nothing else will.

Sometimes, we can be rebellious, having been raised to go our own way and do what we please: 'No one is going to tell me what to do!' If you have this attitude, then you will have problems. When the Holy Spirit speaks to the church and reveals things to the body of Christ, he always brings order and discipline to accomplish his work. We usually enjoy revelation, anointing and power, but dislike order and discipline. However, God wants us to enjoy every aspect.

The apostle's ministry, to a great extent, deals with 'disciplining the disciples' in the body of Christ. The apostle sees how confused and weak things will be otherwise. This might be compared to someone attempting to build a house by tossing bricks into a pile. You can say, 'Now I've built a house,' but your creation lacks order and stability. It may look imposing, but basically it's just a mess. God's works endure. Therefore, they require strength and order. This is why the ministry of the apostle is as essential as the other ministry gifts. You need to understand them and thank God for them.

Every ministry gift, including that of the apostle, can be traced back to Jesus. All of the ministry gifts operated through him. Teaching about these areas of ministry, especially that of the apostle, will not exclude Jesus as some believe because the gifts come from him. He works through them and he receives all the glory from their labours. The one that we honour, lift up, follow and work for is Jesus of Nazareth.

Ministry gifts build the church

The last portion of Ephesians 4:8 says: 'He...gave gifts to men.' 'He' refers to Jesus, who is the one who gives the gifts and places them in the church (1 Cor 12:18). Despite their different functions, the gifts should work together.

First, we need to realise that the ministry gifts are individuals with a task from heaven. They are gifts to the body of Christ and should be accepted as such. Some consider ministry gifts as a threat, while others become confused and uncertain. But if we want to benefit from them, then we must accept them as they are.

We read in the fourth chapter of Ephesians that God wants us to come to a point of spiritual maturity. He wants us to attain to the whole measure of the fullness of Christ, no longer driven by every wind of teaching. The Holy Spirit has the same desire you have for people to be saved and edified, and for God's glory and the works of Jesus to be manifested. He longs to affect the world in a way that makes the kingdom of God visible. This is achieved as the body of Christ is built up through the ministry gifts. However, this is often overlooked, and becomes one of the major causes for the problems and attacks against the body of Christ among the ministry gifts. The enemy strikes here more than anywhere else, because if the ministry gifts don't function as they should, then neither will anything else. They are an inherent part of God's planned and ordained order.

Some people teach that the ministry gifts are unimportant or unnecessary, as long as everyone is functioning well. Everyone needs to be involved in the body of Christ, but this can only happen when the ministry gifts function effectively. 'But this has nothing to do with me! I'm just an ordinary Christian. I'm not called to the ministry gifts.' You're wrong! You still need to recognise God's servants, and discern between true and false in this vital area. You are directly affected whether you have a special calling or not. You need to know and accept how God works through his servants.

Let ministers minister!

Knowledge about the ministry gifts has often been incomplete. We've had vague ideas about the role of a pastor or shepherd. He's the one who runs around wearing himself out, chased by his congregation and his 'brothers'. Then there's the evangelist, who is a little younger than the pastor. You meet him in the church office, sharpening pencils and making copies of the new autumn programme for the youth group and the senior citizens' outing. He longs to be a pastor himself, one day.

Although the above is a comic caricature of the situation in many congregations, nevertheless Satan has perverted the roles of the ministry gifts so that we never understand their function nor allow them to fulfil it. Imagine a plumber coming to your home and hearing you say: 'Do you mind hanging that picture for me?'

'Be glad to,' he replies.

'Would you also take out the rubbish? We've got quite a pile here.'

'Okay,' he says.

'While you're at it, I've been having some trouble with this window. Would you mind fixing it for me?'

'Consider it done.'

'That wall could do with some touching up. How about it?'

'No problem!'

After eight hours, the plumber has done everything except come close to a pipe! You might not even think about this since you're so happy to get everything fixed in your home. He, on the other hand, is feeling extremely frustrated because he is a plumber, and he should be plumbing away! He loves pipes! He thinks pipes! One glance at a pipe and he's checking the flow. Pipes are his life! They are his frame of reference and area of competence. If he never gets the chance to practise his trade because he's taking out his customers' rubbish, moving paintings and fixing windows, he will soon begin to wonder why he's around at all!

Many ministers have never fully entered their calling, simply because they have never been allowed to do so.

You need to understand the ministry gifts

People may have false expectations about the ministry gifts. An evangelist may come to your congregation whom you expect to place an emphasis on teaching the word. The entire time he's preaching, you sit and wonder when he's going to begin teaching. He never does, of course, because an evangelist uses the Bible as a starting point! However, he may simply take a Bible verse, any verse, and start from there: people will be saved, healed, and see signs and wonders! That's the main gift of the evangelist. He needs to be free to function this way. If you try to forge him into an undeviating, systematic Bible teacher, he is likely to be frustrated! Then the Holy Spirit will also be frustrated! Everyone will be frustrated! The same thing will happen if you try to make a Bible teacher into an evangelist.

However, this is a common problem and the reason the body of Christ needs to understand the ministry gifts. We must stop expecting the wrong things and 'pressing the wrong buttons'. People are wonderful, but they always want certain things to take place in their meetings. It's as if they're pressing buttons: 'I want this, I want that!' A minister can recognise this. If it goes too far it becomes witchcraft. Instead, people need to submit their wills to Jesus Christ and say: 'Thy will be done, Lord!' Sometimes people must make a sharp distinction in the spirit between the Lord's servants and those they're serving. Ministers should not be controlled by people's expectations, but by what the Holy Spirit says.

The ministry gifts must be allowed to function in the church according to God's plans and purposes, not only in the local church, but in the entire body of Christ. Only then will the entire body be built up and strengthened.

Your identity is in Jesus – not your ministry

As a Bible teacher, certain expressions of the Holy Spirit's gifts will be evident in your ministry. You have an anointing for your ministry, but also for your responsibilities as a believer. Jesus says that those who believe in him will also do the works that he does (Jn 14:12). This is not referring specifically to the ministry gifts, but to the ministry each believer has. Through the baptism of the Holy Spirit, you receive the anointing necessary to do the works of Jesus! This is why Jesus says that those who believe in him shall cast out evil spirits, speak in new tongues and lay hands on the sick; and they will be made whole (Mk 16:17–18).

Many people desperately want to be something. In the world, many have their identity in their occupation – they are doctors, managing directors, bank managers, bus drivers or whatever. Of course you should enjoy your vocation, but many people have their identities there. If they lose their job, they lose the essence of life itself. This is why many people die soon after retirement.

Your identity as a Christian should never be based on what you do spiritually, but on who you are in Christ Jesus. First and foremost, you are a child of God and not The Great Prophet or Teacher!

Many pastors have a problem with this. Some have the need to be noticed, to be publicly appreciated and someone special. This is only because they haven't yet realised that they are special. Such people are spiritually immature and it would be dangerous for them to have a position of authority. Paul warns against putting new believers into leadership positions, such as head of the church board or pastor (1 Tim 3:6). They can handle neither the responsibility nor the attacks. They fall apart at the slightest resistance because they haven't travelled the road of faith themselves, in their personal circumstances, before receiving the position Jesus intended for them.

No place for human ambition

As a believer, you are to witness about Jesus and do the same works he did. You should do this throughout your life, but there are also specific things Jesus wants you to do. These may not be obvious at first. Therefore, you must allow the Holy Spirit to do a strong work in you. Then, he will be able to do a strong work through you. God will not criticise you, but he tries your heart, your patience and your faith. He knows what you need in the future to withstand the pressure. Therefore, God first removes a false and worldly longing to be something special from our hearts. You can be free from this if you stop identifying yourself as The Great Prophet, The Strong Apostle or the Special Pastor. Try to think this way instead: 'I am a child of God, and I can do the works of Jesus behind the pulpit or behind the wheel of a taxi. It makes no difference. I have no personal ambitions and no hidden ulterior motives. Jesus has set me free!'

There is no place for worldliness, shallowness, vanity or human ambition in the church. You are what Jesus says you are. If he hasn't said anything to you, it doesn't mean that you are worthless, it simply means that he hasn't shown you yet. It doesn't matter whether you know which of the ministry gifts God may have for you. You are a child of God!

Be patient and let God reveal your calling! Don't be impatient or frustrated. People who are always in too much of a hurry are often insecure, selfish or ambitious. They need to appear special, both to themselves and others. Instead, you can rest and be content in the fact that you are accepted by God. Do your best to serve God and if things don't go well, you can always say: 'God, you called me, so please help me.' Then, success won't make you proud and fill you with thoughts of being the most fantastic minister in the world! You're normal and you're simply doing what every believer should do.

Be true to your calling

God will never praise or judge you according to the ministry you had. Instead, he will see how faithful you have been! Suppose God has called you to be an evangelist, but you insist on being a prophet. You prophesy everywhere and have a message for everyone and everything, even if ninety per cent of what you say is completely wrong. You go through life manipulating pastors here and there so that you can come and prophesy in their churches. When you finally get to heaven, you happily expect to receive a prophet's reward. Jesus comes up to you and says: 'Hello, evangelist Smith!'

'Evangelist? I'm a prophet!' you say.

'No,' Jesus replies, 'it's time you received an evangelist's reward, because that's what I called you to be. Unfortunately, it won't be more than fifty pence, because a reward is a reward.'

'Fifty pence for an entire lifetime's work?' you shout.

'You were an evangelist for about twenty minutes during your entire life, so that's what it comes to. I never called you to be a prophet!'

This example may be humorous, but it's very serious to force yourself into a ministry to which you weren't called. It causes problems for yourself, and creates confusion among others.

Therefore, we need to understand and respect the various ministry gifts, and be aware of how they function.

There was a time in Sweden when nearly everyone went around wearing their own ministry label. On some it said 'Apostle' and on others it said 'Prophet'. And on some it didn't simply say 'Prophet' but 'Elijah's Ministry in the Last Days'. There are special ministries in the end times, but not every believer has such a ministry! When people began to grab their own ministries like this, which ones did they choose? Very seldom was it a teacher or a pastor, but rather a prophet or apostle. Suddenly, there were hundreds of 'prophets' and 'apostles'. But God's methods are not like this and not everyone is a leader.

God's call will endure

Let God call you! Who could possibly steal God's call on your life? If you are called by God, then nothing can stop you from becoming what he has decided you should be. But first, you should accept the call and humble your heart before God.

God never regrets his calling. Everyone who has received a calling from heaven has felt rejected by people, but it doesn't matter. Be like Abraham; just stand back and say: 'Help yourself, Lot. Take the plains of Jordan!' Abraham got them eventually, anyway!

God taught me this very clearly while I was studying at the University of Uppsala in Sweden. I knew that I had God's call on my life, but I wasn't exactly sure what form it would take. At that time, I was studying theology with the intention of becoming a priest in the Swedish Lutheran Church, although I could never picture myself in a pastorate! All that I had within me was the desire to pray for people and preach to them, primarily for high school and college students and others in related areas. As graduation approached, I sought the Lord and prayed: 'I don't want to leave Uppsala. I want to witness here and work among the students. You need to perform a miracle!' Suddenly, I received an invitation from a student organisation in Uppsala to be their student pastor! As we discussed the position, I felt that God was in favour of it. They asked me if I would accept the position, but I felt the Holy Spirit told me to refuse it! Then I said to God: 'They'll come back and ask me again if this offer is from you, and then you'll show me if it is from you.'

If something is from God, it will come back! It's much better to draw back than to jump into something rashly! So I held back, and a few weeks later, they called me again. As I waited, the Lord placed Ezekiel 2:4–6 very strongly on my heart:

'The people to whom I am sending you are obstinate and stubborn. Say to them, "This is what the Sovereign Lord says." And whether they listen or fail to listen – for they are a rebellious house – they will know that a prophet has been among them. And you, son of man, do not be afraid of them or their words. Do not be afraid, though briers and thorns are all around you and you live among scorpions. Do not be afraid of what they say or be terrified by them, though they are a rebellious house.'

This is how God spoke to me about Uppsala at that time! When God gave me this message, I understood that he wanted me to accept the offer from the student organisation. I also knew what would happen. Not everyone would listen, but whether they listened or not, they would understand that a prophet had been among them. They called back, and I said 'Yes', because I knew that the offer was from God.

The same is also true for you. You aren't at a department store sale where 'first come, first served' applies. You can be very cautious instead, and let others go first. Jesus will make sure that everything he has placed in your heart will happen! It's better to make it a little harder for God, so that he has to do a few more miracles, than use your flesh to destroy everyone and everything that stands between you and your ministry. Such foolishness and immaturity creates rivalry between ministries and causes a lack of co-operation and flow between the different gifts.

God's ambitions are greater than yours

No gift should operate alone or in isolation, but certain gifts have a greater degree of freedom. Imagine Paul being forced to sit fifteen years in Jerusalem because the group never felt that he was ready to go! God knew what he was doing when he sent Paul away immediately. Paul returned to Jerusalem fourteen years later. He needed the freedom to fulfil his calling. Paul was never isolated nor did he elbow his way ahead in life. He knew his office and his position, and kept fellowship and contact with the ministries around him. He was never tied down nor did he create his own little empire.

The basis for ministry is contentment in Jesus. Personal ambition, individual frustration or uncertainty about God can never be mixed with ministry. If any of these areas are in your life, you will start to magnify yourself and try to prove how fantastic you are. It's much better to let God do that! If God has taken the risk of calling you, then he'll have to accept the consequences.

You are raw material, but if God has called you, he can make something of you. Through him, you will become a vessel that he can use. He prefers to make, use, protect and complete his vessels. God receives all the glory, in the beginning, the middle and the end of your service.

Everything begins in your heart. Even if you serve as an 'ordinary' believer, in a helping capacity, or in some other service mentioned in the Bible, the same principles apply for all. All dissension between ministries originates in insecurity. People then no longer walk in the Spirit, but in the flesh. They have their own ambitions, not God's. God wants you to be pleased with his ambitions, because they are far greater than your own! If you really value your calling, then peace, security, joy and strength in the Holy Spirit will come over your life in a way you have never known before.

When some people are expecting a child, they anticipate a baby of a certain gender. Sometimes, the result isn't what they expected and they are disappointed for months! After having received such a wonderful gift from heaven! The same thing happens to pastors. God tells you to start a church, and you begin to add your own little desires. Later, things aren't what you expected and you wonder what happened. 'But I thought . . .' Stop thinking like this and rejoice instead! Start listening to words from heaven and accept what God is saying to your heart. You'll avoid a lot of frustration this way.

2

The Apostle Lays the Foundation for Lasting Works

Teaching on the ministry gifts is not just an interesting theory, but a vital necessity for all churches. If you refuse to accept what Jesus has called your church to do, then you will always be frustrated.

Since Word of Life Church began, people have always come with the intention of changing our calling. They've tried to introduce different things into the church, but as far as I know, they have never succeeded. We cannot have our own ideas or opinions about God's calling, or alter what he has said. Perhaps you feel that things should be different in your church, but you don't know what may be waiting for you on the other side of the mountain. There might be lions and tigers and bears! God may be doing something on this side of the mountain to prepare for the predators that will turn up later. Meanwhile, you might wonder why things are being done in a certain way. Quite simply, because you may need exactly that when you get to the other side of the mountain! God knows the future, while we walk in the fog of the present!

Mankind is the most ignorant of all creatures. We are often completely ignorant of what God wants to do, yet we're filled with ideas, thoughts and opinions about what may come. God's calling and words must be taken seriously if individual churches, as well as the entire body of Christ, hope to have any kind of future whatsoever. The future lies in the calling and anointing upon the church.

God develops the calling of the church through the ministry gifts. They are different from each other and have varying functions. A carpenter doesn't function like a plumber, who in turn doesn't function like an electrician. A comparison simply cannot be made between the different professions. All of them are needed if you are going to build a garage or a house, but you need to know when each specific skill is needed. If you bring in the electrician first to install the electrical system, then you'll be standing there with wires dangling all around you until the walls are built! Both you and the electrician are going to be thoroughly frustrated with so much unnecessary extra labour. Make sure there are walls before the wiring, but the foundation must be laid before everything else.

Similarly, each ministry gift has a specific task in the process of constructing a solid church. The apostle is like a builder who lays the foundation. Builders don't arrive at the job in a suit and tie, but in a worn pair of overalls. You may have all kinds of opinions about them, but the only thing that matters is whether they lay the foundation. Did they do a good job or did they walk in, throw around a little cement, and then go home again?

Ministry gifts are workers, not a bunch of prima donnas as some may think. If they just kept to themselves, prophesied and prayed for each other, they would end up isolated and completely out of God's will! If one were to gather such a group, it would lack order, be spiritually stagnant, and get nowhere. But, if they were spread out into the harvest fields, what a blessing they could be!

Apostles and prophets lay the foundation for the church

This century has seen increasing revelation on the ministry gifts. We have begun to understand what a pastor is, how an evangelist functions and what a teacher does. However, there are two special gifts that we need to understand so that God can develop strong local churches in the Last Days. There is a fierce struggle concerning these gifts going on right now across the earth. The devil hates strong churches. He tries to crush them, tear them down and render them passive and ineffective. If he can remove the gifts that develop strong local churches, then he'll be satisfied. Apostles and prophets are the gifts that do this more than any others.

The apostle and the prophet are like spearheads, and the church is built on the foundation they lay (Eph 2:20). If they are not allowed to lay a proper foundation, then the church will lose direction, strength, anointing and spiritual insight. You can have good meetings, interesting conferences and fantastic campaigns without these gifts. But when the preachers leave and the crowds disappear, where is the strength that's needed for the local church? If you look closely, you'll see that the church is small, exhausted, confused and unsure of its direction.

The apostle and the prophet, especially the apostle, channel strength to the churches that helps them grow on a daily basis. Churches are not built on conferences, campaigns and seminars. They are built by the steady labour of ordinary people, who are constantly developing and maturing. Maturity, in a biblical sense, refers to increased vigour and stability which makes us stronger. The apostle's ministry is vital and the Bible gives us many examples of this.

The ministry of the apostle – basic and widespread

You are probably aware of the twelve apostles described in the Bible. However, are there apostles today? Some would say 'No'. But if there are prophets, evangelists, pastors and teachers, there must be apostles. Why? Because Jesus himself gave these five gifts to the church. As long as the church is on the earth, and it will be until the Lord returns for it, these gifts will abide. All five of them!

> They devoted themselves to the apostles' teaching and to the fellowship [not the teaching of one apostle, but with the apostles' teaching], to the breaking of bread and to prayer (Acts 2:42).

Here we see how the twelve apostles worked together in laying the foundation for the very first church, the church in Jerusalem. 'But they were unique,' you say. Yes, they were. In Acts 1:21–22, lots were cast to choose a replacement for the Judas who hung himself:

> Therefore it is necessary to choose one of the men who have been with us the whole time the Lord Jesus went in and out among us, beginning from John's baptism to the time when Jesus was taken up from us. For one of these must become a witness with us of his resurrection.

The original twelve apostles were unique because they walked with Jesus from the time of his baptism by John the Baptist, until he rose from the dead. Furthermore, they were eyewitnesses of all that Jesus said and did. Some of the twelve recorded their testimony, which we have in the New Testament today. They were also unique in that they received and communicated revelation, once and for all. Yet the Bible never said that they were the only apostles!

The most important apostle, with the possible exception of Peter, was Paul. He wasn't among the twelve, and constantly had to defend his apostleship against those who would not accept him as an apostle. The most serious attacks Paul faced were the attempts to discredit God's call on his life.

Paul was not one of the original twelve apostles, but nor was Barnabas, who was also called an apostle:

> But when the apostles Barnabas and Paul heard of this, they tore their clothes and rushed out into the crowd, shouting: 'Men, why are you doing this? We too are only men, human like you' (Acts 14:14–15).

The word 'apostles' is clearly stated. It doesn't say 'the apostle Paul and his co-worker Barnabas', it says 'apostles'. In other words, Barnabas was also considered an apostle! In Galatians 1:19, James, the brother of the Lord, is also referred to as one of the apostles. In 1 Thessalonians, Paul writes about the apostolic ministry of Silvanus and Timothy, as well as mentioning Epaphroditus in the letter to the Philippians. There are numerous other examples.

The New Testament appears to identify more apostles than the original twelve. This implies that people functioned as apostles during the lifetimes of the original twelve, without being numbered among them! Therefore, the apostolic ministry must have been widespread and in operation in the church.

The apostolic ministry has long-term effects

We must be set free from the idea of a religious 'St Paul' as portrayed in marble statues, icons and ancient historical images. We must see him in the unique role he had. It was Paul who received the revelation of Jesus' resurrection and wrote one-third of the New Testament. He remains the most important example of a Christian today after Jesus – our primary example.

Paul is an example for us in two areas: first, he shows us how a Christian should live. Church members, as well as those used in ministry gifts, must live lives of consistency. Paul's daily walk and faith demonstrate this.

Second, he exemplifies the ministry of an apostle. He demonstrates the function of an apostle and the results that follow. The book of Acts and the Epistles clearly show Paul's major influence on the early church. Every ministry gift operates within the restrictions of time. The ministry of John the Baptist was effective for only a short period of time, yet his influence was great. Paul not only affected his era, but his influence has remained from generation to generation up to our present day.

An examination of the apostolic ministry will show that its influence continues even after the apostle has died. History speaks of men who weren't called apostles but were in fact just that. Wycliffe was definitely an apostle, as his degree of influence demonstrates. Huss, Luther, Calvin, Knox and Wesley were also apostles. How do we know? From their preaching, their message, their ministry and the enduring legacy they left behind. These are some of the signs of an apostle.

An apostle's ministry is not based on the temporal. Most people, and even shallow Christians, think and live for the moment. However, God always looks at the eternal perspective. This causes most of our trouble, since we're usually preoccupied with ourselves, our problems and what is happening now. We want to be blessed, encouraged and have fun now! God wants this as well, but he has so much more. He always sees things in the eternal framework.

God gives grace for the task

The grace of God relates to two basic areas in the Bible, the first being the 'not guilty' verdict you received for your sins through the grace of Jesus Christ. This verdict set you free from the burden of judgement and condemnation. The second relates to the power or ability God's grace releases.

The Bible frequently mentions the grace of the Lord being with us. You may think that this refers to living with God's pardon upon your life. This is true, but it's only part of the bigger picture. It also means to walk in the grace, power and anointing necessary to complete the task God has given you. Grace gives you the ability to achieve something for God! However, you aren't given grace to do things you shouldn't. If you persist, you'll feel heaviness in the task. The little 'extras' that you or others pile on always weigh you down and pull you away from 'the grace for service' God has given you for your calling. The greater the calling, the greater the grace he gives!

It's quite simple. Both a carpenter and a surgeon need to use a saw, but there is a definite difference in how they use it. A carpenter is never called in to the hospital to amputate legs. He may be able to cut, but he knows nothing about anaesthetics, muscle tissue or stitches. The carpenter and surgeon can use a saw, but the surgeon needs more training to handle his duties. He needs a greater degree of skill. One could also say that there is another level of grace for his task.

Paul wasn't God's favourite, because we are all his favourites. Paul simply received the necessary grace for a delicate task that required a great deal of him. At times, he was faced with incredible attacks, and he called out to God. Second Corinthians 12:8–9 records his threefold cry to God, and the reply that God's grace was sufficient for Paul's needs. The anointing was sufficient for the task.

Follow the heavenly blueprint!

> By the grace God has given me, I laid a foundation as an expert builder, and someone else is building on it. But each one should be careful how he builds (1 Cor 3:10).

Paul calls himself a skilled, or experienced master builder. He was certainly saved and pardoned, but he doesn't say that he's worthless. You'll never hear this kind of talk from Paul, nor has he ever taught anything like it. Instead, he says: 'I'm a skilled master builder. Through God's grace, I can lay a solid foundation.'

The Greek word for 'master builder' means more precisely 'architect'. An architect draws a design or a plan. During Paul's day, the architect was more involved in the building process than architects are today. If someone put a pillar in the wrong place, the architect pointed it out and told the workers to move it. The workers might have even been irritated by the architect because of his continual nagging about the colours, the height of the ceiling and the location of the pillars. 'Can someone move this guy out of the way so that we can work in peace and quiet!' But it's the architect's responsibility to get them to work according to the plans, rather than according to their own ideas. He knows where the pillar has to stand to keep the roof from caving in.

Construction workers only think about the effort required to move the pillar a metre, but an architect has to think further ahead. He knows the importance of precision when you build, and precision requires careful attention to the plans. Everything must be in the right place!

Moses is a good example. The Old Testament describes how he built the tabernacle in the wilderness according to the design given him. Hebrews 8:5 tells how the priests served in a sanctuary that is a copy and shadow of what is in heaven. This is why Moses was warned when he was about to build the tabernacle: 'See to it that you make everything according to the pattern shown you on the mountain.'

This was the revelation Moses received. Compare this with the life and ministry of Paul. He also constantly emphasises that he has received revelation, that he has seen Jesus:

> I want you to know, brothers, that the gospel I preached is not something that man made up. I did not receive it from any man, nor was I taught it; rather, I received it by revelation from Jesus Christ (Gal 1:11–12).

The mission and the message both came through revelation from heaven. He didn't make them up. Paul spent a long time in the Arabian desert searching the Scriptures, and God revealed things to him. What did God reveal? A pattern!

God told Moses to do everything according to the heavenly blueprint. He received the design of God's temple, the tabernacle. Later, Paul received the pattern of God's temple in the Spirit, the church. His life was consumed by the revelation of God's design for his church; what it must consist of, how it was to develop and the dangers it would face. He wasn't just given a doctrine on healing or speaking in tongues, but something that related to the overall picture. The same was true of Moses in the Old Covenant. Moses didn't just receive revelation about the silver fastenings, the vessels or the golden candlestick. He saw it all. He looked into heaven and saw God's revelation for that time.

This is characteristic of the apostle's revelation. A prophet can find the depth of a certain revelation, but the apostle is much broader and more generalised. This is why the Scriptures say in 1 Corinthians 12:28: 'First of all apostles.' The apostle stands on higher ground and sees the entire picture.

God wants order!

Paul's job was to show this heavenly blueprint to believers throughout the world, which meant the Roman Empire. He created conditions for this by preaching the gospel so that people would be saved.

> But thanks be to God that, though you used to be slaves to sin, you wholeheartedly obeyed the form of teaching to which you were entrusted (Rom 6:17).

This pattern creates a dwelling place for God in the Spirit, a temple in which his glory resides. If a man came with a blueprint in his hand and said that he had the pattern for a new temple in which God's glory would dwell, and from which his power would flow, do you know what would happen? The devil would go crazy! Satan constantly attacked Paul because of the abundance of the revelations (2 Cor 12:7). That was the thorn in the flesh that came against him. Satan wanted to rip the pattern into a thousand pieces so that everyone would get wrapped up in their own little piece, leaving the foundation weak and the people divided. Some believers clung to Paul to the exclusion of others, while Peter, Apollos and others received similar treatment. You can read in 2 Corinthians and in the Epistle to the Galatians that people constantly trailed after Paul, tore up what he had done and attempted to destroy and change what he had established. They didn't understand that God had chosen Paul to show them the blueprint for the church.

The devil knows that if apostles and prophets lack the freedom to fulfil their calling, then the church can never be God's spiritual dwelling place. Instead, there will simply be a temporary wave of blessing that will last a few years and then disappear, leaving behind a trail of confusion. Believers should allow themselves to be made into a vessel that can retain the glory! That's why we need apostles today! They build strength and stability into the church. God's presence will then manifest greater than ever before, making it impossible for the gates of hell to prevail against it!

The apostle will become more important than ever in the Last Days, because the devil is going to throw everything he has against the church of the living God. A lack of order in any area makes the church weak, vulnerable and results in defeat. No wonder the apostle loves order and speaks of it continually. Paul says in the Epistle to the Colossians that he rejoices over the order that he sees among them. If a church has order there is no room for the devil! Confusion will leave, and a strong, solid church will remain to welcome in God's glory!

3

The Apostle Makes the Plan a Reality

Consequently, you are no longer foreigners and aliens, but fellow citizens with God's people and members of God's household, built on the foundation of the apostles and prophets, with Christ Jesus himself as the chief cornerstone. In him the whole building is joined together and rises to become a holy temple in the Lord. And in him you too are being built together to become a dwelling in which God lives by his Spirit (Eph 2:19–22).

This verse clearly shows that the church is built on the foundation laid by the apostle and prophet. They are God's master builders and they lay the foundation.

By revelation He made known to me the mystery (as I have briefly written already, by which, when you read, you may understand my knowledge in the mystery of Christ), which in other ages was not made known to the sons of men, as it has now been revealed by the Spirit to His holy apostles and prophets (Eph 3:3–5).

The apostle is God's master builder who constructs God's dwelling in the spiritual realm. This is why Paul often spoke of the church in terms of a temple, a building and dwelling place. These descriptive images were taken from the Old Testament. What God had done for centuries in the Old Covenant would now be taken to the Gentiles. That which only existed in a single nation would now be shared with all nations. This is why God instituted the ministry gifts – to reveal the heavenly blueprint. Through the ministry gifts, the pattern would be transferred in a way that would keep the Gentiles from confusion, and the final product from becoming something God did not want. God used the ministry gifts to make a way for the newly saved Gentiles to enter a spiritual dwelling place, just as the Jews entered the temple in Jerusalem. God's presence remained in the temple until the beginning of the New Covenant. Then, all that the Old Testament temple in Jerusalem was, in the physical realm, the New Testament church became in the spiritual realm.

You need to have a spiritual understanding of the way God builds. He gives a pattern to each individual church through the Holy Spirit. This does not mean a church that consists of ministry gifts parading around to the applause of onlookers. Instead, we should all work together so that the glory of God will be seen in our land. When you submit to this in your heart, you will then realise your purpose and become a productive member of the body of Christ. And you'll enjoy every minute of it!

Remember that you are involved in something much larger than yourself. The circumstances in which you are placed will only be as strong as you are in faith. Walk in the Spirit, know and love Jesus and defeat the things that come against you! Then you will be a strong stone in the temple wall, providing support on every side. You'll be joined together with others to become a spiritual dwelling place for the glory of God! And everything will be in total accord with the heavenly pattern.

Two pitfalls – individualism and collectivism

The temple in the Old Covenant was built by meticulous individuals. They didn't arrive in the morning, yawning, throw around a little cement, drink some coffee and then head home early because it was Monday and they were tired. Neither did they forget their tools, and wait three weeks to return with them. These things just didn't happen. Instead there was an attention to detail, order, revelation, holiness and purity. There was a purpose to what they were doing, and each individual was aware of his task. This is what God wants to see in the body of Christ today!

There are two traps into which anyone may fall. First, there is extreme individualism, where 'everyone did as he saw fit' (Judg 21:25). Each person is his own king and builds his own kingdom. The second pitfall is the concentration of power to a group of individuals. This results in man's control rather than the Holy Spirit's leading.

God doesn't want you to end up in either of these two traps. He wants you to be led by the Holy Spirit as an individual as well as in a group. Only the stability and direction of the Holy Spirit will bring the results God intends. The wind blows where it will, but that doesn't mean that we should move along like a wind-blown leaf!

The Spirit chooses whoever he wants

The temple in the Old Covenant originated through the inspiration of the Holy Spirit. He provided a pattern of the temple for David and Solomon, exactly as Moses received a pattern for the tabernacle in the wilderness. Those who worked on the tabernacle were also anointed by the Holy Spirit:

> So Bezalel, Oholiab and every skilled person to whom the Lord has given skill and ability to know how to carry out all the work of constructing the sanctuary are to do the work just as the Lord has commanded (Exod 36:1).

Hebrews 8:5 describes how God spoke to Moses about doing everything according to the heavenly pattern. The same is true of the workmen who received wisdom and understanding from the Holy Spirit for their tasks.

Perhaps Bezalel wanted the Holy Spirit to anoint him to travel and preach on the other side of the world. When God spoke to him about twining linen, he probably wondered what was going on. But the Holy Spirit chooses the person, the method and the task. When he chooses you to do something, you will enjoy doing it. Do you know what else will happen when the Holy Spirit comes upon you? You'll begin to understand how to do it!

If a person involved in spiritual work is never inspired, creative or full of initiative but complains instead, then it's time to question whether the individual has the anointing for that task. If you believe you're called to be an intercessor, but you don't want to be one and find it boring, then you should ask yourself whether you really are called to be one. If you are, then you need to ask yourself if you have accepted your calling.

The Holy Spirit will come upon you when you accept your calling. If you are an intercessor, you will think, sleep and live intercessory prayer. You will constantly be aware of your calling and desire to develop and be made more effective. If God has called you to be a pastor, you'll start to think like a pastor. 'How can I take care of these people? How can I develop this work?' If you are a musician, you'll start receiving melodies from the Holy Spirit. There will be an explosion of creativity in the body of Christ! But it cannot begin until the ministry gifts are in place.

Let the Holy Spirit do the organising!

The apostle activates other ministries through the anointing over him. He encourages the gifts that are present in others. He corrects, develops and puts people to work. The result is a team that works together in their shared wisdom and anointing, just like Bezalel and Oholiab!

God wants the church to be a dynamic workplace, which edifies the body of Christ and proclaims the gospel to the world. Believers should be working together rather than seeking their own glory. The Old Covenant temple was constructed by skilled, anointed workmen. Moses was not the only one who was anointed! Bezalel, Oholiab and the rest of the workmen were given the anointing necessary for the task. In the same way, all believers are anointed to build up the body of Christ, God's dwelling place in the Spirit. They preach, encourage, witness, pray for the sick and do whatever the Holy Spirit wants them to do.

When every one of us does what Jesus asks, then there will be a co-ordination through the Holy Spirit. Exodus 40 says that when the parts of the temple were finished, Moses put them together.

Every object had a purpose. The tabernacle, and all its contents, were then sanctified and prepared for use by the sprinkling of the blood.

You must delegate!

God gave the pattern to Moses, who in turn told the people what to do. The Spirit then fell upon those who were willing to work. Moses was with them, and supervised, but the people did the actual work. Moses later took the finished parts and assembled them as God had instructed. If the workers hadn't accepted this order of doing things, then there would never have been a tabernacle. Oholiab might have said: 'I've worked on this, and now Moses wants to take the credit for what I've done! The boys in the shop did the work while the guys from administration are out playing golf. And Moses just sits and mumbles in his tent the entire time!'

This could have happened, but fortunately it didn't! Many churches have this problem, which is rooted in selfishness. Sectarianism begins like this, too. Everyone has a job to do, but it neither starts nor ends there! You reach a point where you have to let go of what you have done. If you don't do it voluntarily, then God will take it from you. It's much better to say: 'Thank you for this, Jesus. It's all yours!'

Paul called himself a skilled master builder. He knew exactly how to lay the foundation, but he also allowed others to get involved in the work:

> According to the grace of God which was given to me, as a wise master builder I have laid the foundation, and another builds on it. But let each one take heed how he builds on it (1 Cor 3:10 NKJV).

Here, Paul is referring to the foundation laid for the church in Corinth. This shows the greatness in him. He could have stayed in Ephesus or Corinth and not let go of his life's work. But everything that grows must be left to do just that. This doesn't mean that Paul abandoned a church, because he repeatedly returned to help it develop. He kept informed of what was happening and wrote to them to correct or encourage them, until he reached a point where he had to let go. Others came and built on the foundation he had laid. Having completed the foundation, Paul continued in his calling, trusting that others would carry on where he left off. Paul knew what to do, but he also knew where the boundaries were set.

Paul's goal – to build up the body of Christ

Many believe that it's sufficient to have Jesus as Saviour, and preach about healing and salvation. But although it's wonderful to go out and preach about Jesus, this alone is not sufficient. It would result in a group of healed and saved people, but also a lot of confusion. God wants a church!

There has been much teaching about evangelism and a victorious personal life, but not enough about how the Holy Spirit challenges, raises up and perfects the local church. It's not enough to have people prophesy here and there. The entire church needs to become spiritually mature. Although Paul evangelises, he basically does one thing – he builds up the body of Christ!

Paul's writings deal very little with evangelism. His letters focus almost exclusively on building up the church. The work really begins when people get saved! These new believers are the raw material from which God builds his temple.

People must be strengthened in their faith, become spiritually mature and come into the task to which God has called them. But it cannot happen until the ministry gifts are accepted and allowed to edify believers and help them in their work. Every believer has a vital part to play, while giving support to others. Selfishness and egotistic thinking disappear as the believer grows strong in the Lord. Each believer must be built up if the local church is to have a strong flow of the Holy Spirit that won't fade outside the pulpit. You need more than eloquent sermons and shouts of encouragement! The anointing of the Holy Spirit has to meet people's needs and defeat the attacks of the devil in their lives. Then they will grow in the Lord.

When the ministry gifts are accepted and allowed to function, we will have strong, spiritually mature churches that can see in the spirit and discern what is from the Holy Spirit. When God is in his temple – the church of the living God – flesh begins to shake and tremble. Believers will no longer be thrown back and forth with every wind of doctrine. They will be alert and discerning, strong, free and pure, with the fear of God in their lives. The church will be fit for use, filled with love, unity and freedom. This is where we are headed!

In the Last Days, God is going to restore doctrine, spiritual life, power and order. This includes order among the ministry gifts in the local church and in the body of Christ. Then we will all be joined into God's dwelling in the Spirit.

4

The Apostle – a Pioneer

In Jesus, the head of the church, we see all five of the ministry gifts. He was an evangelist and prophet, as well as the Good Shepherd. He also sat and taught the people, as does a teacher. In Hebrews 3:1, he is called 'the Apostle and High Priest of our confession' (NKJV). The word 'apostle' means 'sent' or 'sent out'. Jesus was certainly sent! He was sent from heaven to bring salvation to you and me. The gifts of the Spirit, the fruits of the Spirit and the ministry gifts were contained in the anointing on Jesus' life and ministry.

The most important ministry is the believer's. This was the last thing Jesus spoke about as he sent out the disciples (Mk 16:15–18). Every believer has this ministry, and it contains elements from every ministry gift.

For example, a believer should prophesy. Paul says in 1 Corinthians that all can prophesy as long as it is done in order (14:31). The gift of prophecy in your life doesn't necessarily mean that you are a prophet. However, you can still be used in prophecy and participate in what it means to be a prophet. In addition, you are also sent out and need to take the initiative, which is part of being an apostle. You should witness, which is part of the evangelist's calling, as well as care for others, which is the pastor's calling. Finally, you are to instruct and edify those around you, which is part of the teacher's ministry. As a Spirit-filled believer, you participate in every ministry Jesus had.

Jesus says that those who believe in him will do the works that he did (Jn 14:12). Never say that you're only an insignificant believer, and that you would really love to be an apostle. You are a complete child of God, a complete servant of the Lord! When Saul was saved, an ordinary believer came and ministered to him, not an apostle. Ananias, from Damascus, was a brother filled with the Holy Spirit and with the gift of prophecy. Led by the Holy Spirit, Ananias came to Saul, set him free from his blindness and prayed for him.

Ananias was an ordinary believer, just like you. An apostle who would shake the entire world was born because God used an 'ordinary' believer. That's why you should never depreciate the ministry of the believer. It is the greatest and strongest ministry and will be used more than any other in the end times. Rejoice and be content if you have the ministry of a believer!

The apostle's anointing flows through all the ministries

The fingers on your hand provide a simple illustration of the different ministry gifts:

The index finger represents the prophet, whose task is to point out the direction. The prophet points at the spiritual condition of the church, reveals sin and shows which road to take: 'This is the way; walk in it' (Is 30:21).

The middle finger represents the evangelist, who reaches further than the others. An evangelist is most content out in the field and less content within the confines of a sanctuary. An evangelist should not be limited to travelling between churches, but needs to be equipped by the church and then sent out beyond it. Otherwise, he'll be extremely frustrated.

The ring finger represents the pastor's ministry, for he has an almost marital relationship with the church he serves. A shepherd loves his flock, takes care of it, encourages it and meets its spiritual needs.

The little finger is the ministry of the teacher. Some jokingly say that the little finger is small enough to get the wax out of your ears, making it easier to hear what is being said!

The thumb symbolises the apostle. It's a little stronger than the other fingers and vital if the hand is to grip anything. It can also touch the other fingers. This simply means that when the apostle needs to be an evangelist, a prophet or any of the others, he can. The apostle's anointing flows into all of the other ministries when needed. There is a stability and flexibility in the apostle that is necessary for the body of Christ to grow, mature and be strong in the Lord.

The church needs all the ministry gifts

The devil wants the church to be weak, divided, confused and without revelation. If there aren't any prophets, then there won't be revelation knowledge in the church. If there are no evangelists, then the church will lack the evangelistic fervour needed to go out and win souls. If there are no teachers, then there won't be any revelational instruction. Without apostles, there will be no foundation, structure, stability or leadership. All these areas of ministry are needed! Otherwise, neither the individual Christian nor the church could come to a place of spiritual maturity.

The Bible never mentions cardinals, popes and archbishops, but a great deal is said about apostles and prophets. God doesn't want a rigid, hierarchical system of control in the church. He wants his own ministers. Then he will release a flood of individuals who can be used as ministry gifts. They will serve the local church and the body of Christ with revelation and the presence and power of God. The church has often done itself a disservice by only receiving what it personally wants, while stopping everything else. But the time for this has passed.

Jesus is the centre, but his ministry extends through the ministry gifts to bless people. If you accept the anointing over a certain area of ministry, then you participate in the gift God expresses through it. Nevertheless, you should still receive directly from heaven yourself. You are responsible for your own life and can hear what the Holy Spirit is saying to you. You don't have to be old to hear from heaven. You may be young, like Samuel. He didn't recognise the Lord's voice at first, but he learned. When Samuel was six or seven years old, God spoke to him. He gave him a prophecy that dealt with the entire country, the service of the priests, and the direction that God's people should take. God does what he wants, with whoever he wants.

The apostle is a pioneer

The apostolic ministry does not start immediately. Paul was called to the apostolic ministry after having served a time as a teacher and prophet in the church at Antioch. He wasn't in an apostolic ministry from the beginning, although he was called to be one from his mother's womb. It's one thing to be called, and another to be separated for the calling. The third step is to be sent, and the fourth is to be effective!

Perhaps deep in your heart you know, or think you know, what God wants you to be. But mostly you haven't a clue! Did you know ten years ago what you would be doing now? Probably you couldn't have imagined it in your wildest dreams. It's more than you could have thought or prayed for, isn't it? Don't fix your mind on one thing, because you might be disappointed! God chooses the people for the job and places them into service for him. He has chosen to set apostles first in the church. They are spread across the earth and in every generation, because God has a task for every generation.

It isn't a question of hierarchy. When 1 Corinthians 12:28 states, 'first apostles' (NKJV), the word implies that God uses the apostle to go first. More than any other ministry, the apostle is a pioneer. Paul felt restless in Jerusalem. He didn't go there until the Holy Spirit urged him to, and that was not until fourteen years after he had begun his work. He was then forced to go to Jerusalem because of some problems, but he was never comfortable there. Why? Because he wasn't the first one there! He wasn't so remarkable. He just had the heart of a pioneer.

The apostle ploughs new ground

> We, however, will not boast beyond proper limits, but will confine our boasting to the field God has assigned to us, a field that reaches even to you ... Neither do we go beyond our limits by boasting of work done by others. Our hope is that, as your faith continues to grow, our area of activity among you will greatly expand, so that we can preach the gospel in the regions beyond you. For we do not want to boast about work already done in another man's territory (2 Cor 10:13,15–16).

God called Paul to be an apostle to the Gentiles. Jesus came to him and said: 'I will send you to the Gentiles.' Paul set out and preached across the Roman Empire. There were other apostles out doing the same thing, even if most of them stayed longer in Jerusalem. But eventually they were dispersed, and started to preach and conquer new areas. They must have run into each other at times! We know from the letter to the Galatians that Paul met Peter, not in Jerusalem but in Antioch, as well as in other places.

Paul says: 'I won't build on someone else's foundation. My ministry is to lay new foundations, so I won't go to places to lay double foundations. If Peter has established something in one place, then I'll go somewhere else.' It's more common for people to do the exact opposite: 'Have you been there? Well then, I'll go there too!' Very few say: 'Have you been there? Well then, I'll just go somewhere else.' The apostle, however, is driven to plough new land and conquer new territories.

> It has always been my ambition to preach the gospel where Christ was not known, so that I would not be building on someone else's foundation. Rather, as it is written: 'Those who were not told about him will see, and those who have not heard will understand' (Rom 15:20–21).

Can you imagine a better pioneer? Some people look for a church where they can be members and perhaps be 'discovered'. They feel they have a prophetic or apostolic ministry. Please, don't do this! If you have such a calling, look for some wilderness where the gospel has yet to be preached. This pioneer spirit really needs to come upon us. In Sweden, we have a Viking heritage! We need to be set free from the worldliness of the Vikings, and stir up their positive attributes. When spring came, they launched their boats and said: 'So long, see you in a few years!' Off they went on a new Viking adventure. We need that same pioneer spirit in us!

The apostle has a strong desire to do something that no one else has ever done. Paul had neither a newsletter nor a camera. He had no pictures to send home, nor was this the purpose of his work. His intention was to establish the gospel, God's power and kingdom in places where the name of Christ was earlier unknown.

Closed doors can't stop you!

When I was studying at the University of Uppsala, I remember hearing our archbishop say that our district, Uppland, was extremely difficult.

'There's probably never been a real revival here,' he said.

'Then there will be,' I thought!

Most places and people are sluggish and hard to get started. You'll never get out of bed in the morning if you're driven by your feelings. You simply need to make up your mind!

If you don't have an open door for an outreach, then remember that Paul didn't either for most of the time. All the doors were closed in Damascus. Paul would still be sitting there today if he listened to some charismatic teaching that says you shouldn't go until the door is open. Do you know what Paul did? He went right through the doors and was lowered down the wall in a basket. Closed doors were never a problem for Paul.

Consider Jericho! Think what would have happened if Joshua had said: 'Well, the doors are closed. We must have missed God's will somewhere along the way.' But Joshua was right in the centre of God's will, and that's why the doors were closed. The devil was scared to death!

There isn't a door that won't open and a wall that won't fall if God so wills. Get some of Paul's pioneer spirit instead of a restless attitude. When you meet resistance or something comes against you, don't take root and get stuck. Think about new conquests instead, like Paul. Paul made it a matter of honour not to preach the gospel where the name of Jesus was already known:

... so that I would not be building on someone else's foundation. Rather, as it is written: 'Those who were not told about him will see, and those who have not heard will understand.'

This is a real apostle!

As mentioned earlier, the apostolic ministry contains elements of the other ministry gifts within it. The apostle may be used in all of them, depending on the need at the time and the gifts of the Spirit. There are examples of apostles who were strong pastors or teachers, while others had a prophetic or evangelistic emphasis. They had all of the gifts, but some were more prevalent than others. It is difficult to say which gift was strongest in Paul, but here we see him as the evangelist: 'I must reach those who have never heard!'

Be driven by your spirit

Why don't people go out and preach or witness? Because they don't have a heart for the lost. I'm talking about believers. They've received a new heart, but still allow the flesh to rise up and choke the life on the inside. How did God speak to Paul? Paul said: 'For God is my witness, whom I serve with my spirit in the gospel of his Son' (Rom 1:9 NKJV).

Paul didn't serve God from his flesh. He was driven and motivated by his spirit. You can have the same kind of motivation. If you do, you'll never burn out, lag behind or become passive. Paul was like a lion, always hungry for new prey:

I long to see you so that I may impart to you some spiritual gift to make you strong – that is, that you and I may be mutually encouraged by each other's faith. I do not want you to be unaware, brothers, that I planned many times to come to you (but have been prevented from doing so until now) in order that I might have a harvest among you, just as I have had among the other Gentiles. I am bound both to Greeks and non-Greeks, both to the wise and the foolish. That is why I am so eager to preach the gospel also to you who are at Rome (Rom 1:11–15).

Paul had never been to Rome when he wrote the letter to the Romans. He simply longed to go there; he had to go there. He felt he had something to impart that Rome didn't have, but needed. The same is true for preachers today. It would be a waste of time to travel to a church and preach where others have preached, just to fill your schedule. There needs to be a better reason.

Always new areas

But now that there is no more place for me to work in these regions, and since I have been longing for many years to see you, I plan to do so when I go to Spain. I hope to visit you while passing through and to have you assist me on my journey there, after I have enjoyed your company for a while. Now, however, I am on my way to Jerusalem in the service of the saints there (Rom 15:23–25).

Paul is always on the move. Do you know what was burning inside him? New conquests! Don't lock an apostle in a cage, because he'll become like a lion in a zoo – toothless and lazy. He has an area in which he must work. He doesn't want to intrude on someone else's area, but keeps to the area given him by God. His boast is in the Lord.

Paul worked throughout the Roman Empire. There were other apostles working there as well, but that didn't keep Paul from being bold. Romans 15 recounts how he preached in Achaia, in Macedonia and even in Illyricum (former Yugoslavia). To reach Illyricum from Greece, he had to travel through Albania. It's likely that he preached there as well.

This was Paul's ministry. Yet he never travelled around like a restless ghost. He remained in each city until his work was completed. He was in Corinth for eighteen months, and at least two years in Ephesus. He stayed in Caesarea for two years as well, but not voluntarily, since he was in prison! Paul never worked half-heartedly. He came and did what he was supposed to do, achieving a work that lasted for generations.

5

Paul Understood the Power of Repentance

The ministry of the apostle, like that of the prophet, has been surrounded by conflicting ideas and opinions. This is hardly surprising, because these gifts can be quite special and spectacular. Some individuals have incorrectly proclaimed themselves as prophets, apostles or another ministry gift, but this shouldn't stop us from teaching about them. Never be afraid to mention or examine a subject the Bible deals with simply because it's controversial! Some get nervous when they hear the word 'demon', although Jesus often spoke about them.

The devil distorts biblical truths which have become the object of abuse or unsound practice. He does this to scare Christians and rob them of revelation that could be a great blessing. It seems that the Holy Spirit has to wait to deal with certain controversial topics. Some subjects have become so 'hot' that it's difficult to figure out what is involved.

What is a controversial topic? It's any topic that is new and relatively unknown. These topics usually give room to all kinds of opinions. We need to deal with these subjects with faith and follow what Jesus said to Martha: 'Did I not tell you that if you believed, you would see the glory of God?' (Jn 11:40).

Be open, rather than closed and full of fear, or you won't get anywhere in the kingdom of God.

The ministry of the apostle has also been abused. There are many examples of self-proclaimed apostles claiming authority over churches they neither established nor had anything to do with. They visit churches claiming to be an apostle and start to point out everything under the sun. Paul never acted this way! He did proclaim and correct, but he also had a relationship with those churches. Paul was involved in helping individuals. First Thessalonians describes the gentleness in the relationship he had with them, 'like a mother caring for her little children' (2:7). He encouraged and challenged them as a father, spoke to them on a personal level and also preached for the crowds. Paul's flexibility is still an example of how an apostle should act.

We are not saying that someone should come in the flesh, take a ministry position for himself and use it to control others. Instead, we are referring to the gifts Jesus has given and God has intended for his work with individuals.

Everything God says about ministries and order is there to bless and help us. God wants the body of Christ, the church, to survive. He wants it to be strong and grow. The local church should never be bound or controlled, but rather grow steadily and deal with its own responsibilities. Neither should it move in fear. God wants us all to come into an even greater freedom.

A greater perspective

The apostle and prophet have more of a long-term perspective than the other ministries in the body of Christ.

The prophet can see far ahead, perhaps thousands of years ahead, as we see with the Old Testament prophets. They can also speak about events in the near future. The prophet Agabus spoke of a famine which came to pass in the days of Claudius (Acts 11:28). Agabus then prophesied over Paul concerning what would happen to him when he reached Jerusalem (Acts 21:10–11). A prophet can speak to individuals as well as about 'the bigger picture'.

The prophet has the ability to see the future. He is, as the Old

Testament expresses, a seer – one who sees. His spiritual eyes are open and he sees. This should be true of us all. But if there is anyone who can see and hear spiritual things, it is the prophet! He is our guide. We should listen when he speaks, because God's word says that we will prosper when we listen to his prophets (2 Chron 20:20).

The apostle also sees with an eternal perspective. He is a strategist, and surveys the battlefield like a general. When the ordinary soldier only sees a mound of clay, a hill or bulwark to conquer, the general sees the entire battlefield and the purpose for each battle. He knows what is simultaneously happening at different locations. He has a far-reaching ability that enables him to lead the army into victory. The apostle and the general view events from high above, like an eagle.

The apostle and prophet are those ministries in the body of Christ that are most attacked. The devil doesn't want them to see and hear! If they do not proclaim what God is saying, then people might not listen when confronted by their words. People may wonder if their words will really come to pass, or they may not like what they hear and ignore it. We can have as many opinions as we want, but when instruction comes from heaven, we need to listen, otherwise we'll get nowhere and become passive.

Conversion – complete commitment

What is conversion? Conversion isn't joining a church or trying to act like a Christian! It isn't something we pick up and try, to see if it works! Conversion is a total abandonment of the old life! God by his Spirit destroys the 'old man'. Then he creates a new person just for himself. From the moment you are born again, you are reserved completely for God.

Most believers act as if they were free. They say that Jesus has made them free, and he has. He made them free to be slaves! Does this sound strange to you? Romans 1:1 refers to 'Paul, a servant of Christ Jesus'. The word in the original Greek means 'slave': 'Paul, a slave of Jesus Christ.' Conversion means that you have given up your own will and ambitions. God is all you live for, because he is the only one you are interested in.

Some say that Paul's opposition to Jesus, prior to being saved, made it easier for him. 'I was never against Jesus earlier, so it's more difficult for me to be actively for him,' some people say. What nonsense! We can all be radically for Jesus, since we all participate in the same conversion. God wants everyone to undergo the same kind of conversion as Paul! There must be a clear line drawn between darkness and light, life and death. There needs to be a definite turning point when revelation enters your life. It can come in many different ways, but when it does, you'll know.

A debt of gratitude to Jesus

When you study the life of Paul, you'll see that something grabbed him, shook him and changed his life. It was his conversion. At the moment of conception, God gives a child its full potential. The same is true of the spiritually newborn. In the book of Acts, Paul constantly refers to his conversion. The real reason for Paul's success was that he was genuinely converted.

'Not everyone can fall off a horse on the road to Damascus!' you might say. No, but every heart can repent! Sometimes, preaching about conversion is superficial. It's not enough to pray a prayer of salvation if you haven't changed deep inside, if you haven't been powerfully confronted with the reality of sin, righteousness and judgement. If this is the case, it won't be long before you begin to grumble and end up backsliding. Sometimes, one can question whether the person was ever really saved, or converted. When a person is truly converted, a reaction similar to Paul's takes place. One feels a debt of gratitude to Jesus for what he has done. 'I must do something for him, because he has done so much for me!'

'We all fell to the ground, and I heard a voice saying to me in Aramaic, "Saul, Saul, why do you persecute me? It is hard for you to kick against the goads." Then I asked "Who are you, Lord?" "I am Jesus, whom you are persecuting," the Lord replied. "Now get up and stand on your feet. I have appeared to you to appoint you as a servant and as a witness of what you have seen of me and what I will show you. I will rescue you from your own people and from the Gentiles. I am sending you to them'" (Acts 26:14–17).

Paul asked: 'Who are you, Lord?' When he was born again, he received an immediate reply to that question, because Jesus revealed it to him. We should also do this first. 'God, I don't know you. I've been saved, but who are you? I have no understanding of you. Show yourself to me! How can I live for you, love you and follow you if I don't even know who you are?'

Paul's next question soon followed. 'What shall I do, Lord?' (Acts 22:10). Paul began his new life at this point. He didn't start with questions like: 'How often do I have to go to meetings? How much do I have to help? Do I have to tithe? Do I really have to speak in tongues?' These questions never existed in Paul's mind. His conversion and the life he lived had another quality to them. God doesn't want only a few ministers to achieve this level of relationship with him. He wants the entire church to live in it.

Paul – an example in intercession

The greatness in Paul's life wasn't his travelling, preaching or meeting with the Emperor. Neither was it being stoned, left for dead only to rise up and return to town. These weren't the areas of Paul's greatness. They were the results of his greatness.

First, the greatness in Paul's life and service was his total commitment to the one who saved him. Second, it related to his prayer life. There is no greater example, with the exception of Jesus himself, of a person committed to prayer as Paul. He prayed constantly! It is easy to learn where people are in their spiritual life by how much they pray. What relationship do they have with Jesus? Do they have a relationship with their own thoughts, or do they live with Jesus daily?

Paul never let his captivity hinder his work. He wrote letters and prayed. He continued to work and fruit came as a result. He did what he was supposed to, whether he was personally present among the people or not. When writing to the Christians in

Colosse, a church he hadn't visited, he acknowledged that neither of them knew each other. Despite this, he had been with them in spirit and rejoiced over the order that was present there (Col 2:5). How could he do this? Through prayer.

Paul rarely prayed for himself, except when he asked for the prayers of others to open doors for him to preach the gospel. He continually prayed for the churches and that the kingdom of God would increase. How could he commit his entire life to doing this? Because he was truly saved!

Four areas of the apostolic ministry

Paul's conversion is described in Acts chapters 9, 22 and 26. Reading from Acts 9:5, we see the following:

Paul, or Saul, hears the voice of Jesus: 'I am Jesus, whom you are persecuting' (v. 5). He falls from his horse, is led into Damascus, doesn't eat or drink for three days, and then Ananias comes. Ananias had a vision in which Jesus told him to go to the street called 'straight', to the house of Judas, where there was a man from Tarsus named Saul, 'for he is praying' (v. 11). Ananias then says that he has heard many talk about the evil Saul has done to the Christians. This is what his mind tells him. Jesus answers and tells him not to worry:

> 'This man is my chosen instrument to carry my name before the Gentiles and their kings and before the people of Israel. I will show him how much he must suffer for my name' (Acts 9:15–16).

Here, we see Jesus state the four directions Paul's ministry is to take. First, he names the groups to which Paul is to take his name: Gentiles, kings and the children of Israel. Finally, Jesus speaks about Paul's conversion and its consequences.

I believe this applies not only to Paul's calling, but to any apostolic calling. The apostolic ministry always operates in the following four areas:

1. A call to the Gentiles: To get people saved and establish new churches.

2. A call to speak to kings and authorities: Paul had much contact with kings and leaders. It's true that many contacts were made in a court of law where he was on trial, but they were none the less contacts.

In Jerusalem and Caesarea, Paul took the name of Jesus before the authorities. He spoke before Felix, Festus, Agrippa and the high priests. Surprisingly, they weren't saved! One might call this a failure, but Paul did what he was supposed to and gave those listening the same opportunity. Agrippa was close to becoming a Christian (Acts 26:28).

Jesus came to Paul in a vision and told him that he would be going to Rome to present the name of Christ there also. It appears that the Emperor was never saved, but we know that Paul presented the name of Jesus to him. From this point on, we know that Paul succeeded in influencing the spiritual atmosphere of the entire Roman Empire.

3. A call to the children of Israel: Paul bore deep within his heart God's plan of salvation for the Jewish people. As an apostle, he could never forget this. He reserved three chapters in his letter to the Romans for this purpose, and mentioned it repeatedly.

4. A calling to commitment: 'I will show him how much he must suffer for my name' (Acts 9:16).

Commitment is the response to a calling from God. The stronger the commitment to God's calling, the better the ministry. The better the ministry, the greater the suffering. This is not a case of substitutionary suffering someone else endures for you. Neither does this refer to the sufferings of Jesus, which are completely different. The word says, 'Everyone who wants to live a godly life in Christ Jesus will be persecuted' (2 Tim 3:12). You can't escape it! You shouldn't be afraid of persecution, but you should be aware and prepared for it.

Many Christians suffer the delusion of a 'comfortable' Christian life. They would gladly be prophets or apostles, have a strong anointing and do the miraculous works of Jesus. The problem is that they want it all wrapped up with beautiful wrapping paper, so that everyone will like them and keep them out of trouble for the sake of the gospel. Today, some Christians are suspicious of persecution and suffering, implying that those who suffer persecution must have done something wrong. However, the opposite is true. There are many verses in the Bible that show you encounter resistance when you do something right!

Many passages show that wherever Paul went, he upset someone! Nearly everything he did led to confrontation. There were screaming mobs, stone throwing, furious 'little old ladies' (it says in Acts 13:50 that the Jews stirred up the foremost women of the town) and hysterical high priests. Chaos broke loose wherever he set foot! We don't always see this when we read the book of Acts. Instead, we dive into the verses that speak of blessing, but we need to read the context before and after those verses. Hell gets stirred up when you have something from heaven. You need to understand this!

I believe that these four areas are indicators of an apostolic ministry. Furthermore, the apostolic ministry results in strong churches where people get saved. But the result of commitment is also persecution for the sake of Jesus' name. This is an inherent part of the apostolic ministry, and something we cannot ignore.

You must get serious

In Acts 9:19–20, we read that Paul has now been saved and has spent time with the disciples in Damascus. The Bible says that he began to preach immediately! He didn't wait until fifteen years after his conversion, but started right away. In the letter to the Galatians, Paul describes himself this way:

> For you have heard of my previous way of life in Judaism, how intensely I persecuted the church of God and tried to destroy it. I was advancing in Judaism beyond many Jews of my own age and was extremely zealous for the traditions of my fathers. But when God, who set me apart from birth and called me by his grace, was pleased to reveal his Son in me so that I might preach him among the Gentiles, I did not consult any man (Gal 1:13–16).

Paul was neither self-indulgent nor obstinate. His life was immediately consecrated to the mission to which Jesus had called him.

Therefore, he asked no one for advice, but left straight away. This is typical of an apostle's initiative. If apostles through the centuries had taken time to seek the advice of other people, the devil would have stolen what God had given them. God knew that this would even have happened with Paul.

I lost all of my friends when I was saved. They thought I was crazy, because when I got saved, I got saved! Immediately, I started to tell them all about Jesus. You need to be just as radical in your conversion. You have to get serious. You can't simply plan how you're going to live your own life; that you'll go to Bible school, get a job and get married. God has called you, not to a life of comfort, but to a life like Paul's – a missionary on fire for God! He says:

> I have worked much harder . . . Besides everything else, I face daily the pressure of my concern for all the churches (2 Cor 11:23, 28).

This is what God has for you. He wants you to be a labourer. Start right now! The Holy Spirit has touched your heart, and now your life is focused on only one thing: to do what God called you to when you were saved. You need to be prepared, equipped, and then run your race.

Paul knew his calling

The detailed account of Paul's conversion in Acts indicates the revelation that came to him as a newborn child of God. Jesus says to Paul: 'You are a chosen instrument, Paul. You are to take forth my name.'

Paul was not supposed to present his own name, although he knew who he was. For example, he never writes: 'A little unknown brother is writing to you. I'm not even sure where I come from.' Instead he says:

> Paul, an apostle – sent not from men nor by man, but by Jesus Christ and God the Father, who raised him from the dead (Gal 1:1).

Paul isn't bragging or self-centred. Paul speaks about Jesus and presents him, while being secure in his own identity.

It's just the same for you. Realise that you have a ministry, a calling, an anointing. You should know who you are! Of course, you shouldn't be egocentric and say: 'I have seen, I have heard!' In Paul's letters, the word 'I' appears hundreds of times, but it's not noticeable because Jesus is the focus of his writings. Although Paul continually speaks about himself, there is no self-centredness. Paul was marked by his calling from the very beginning. Whether he says the name of Jesus or not, Jesus always shines forth through him!

Accept your calling

The influence of the apostolic ministry does not immediately appear in large headlines. While other ministries think in terms of hours, days and weeks, the apostle thinks in terms of months, years and decades. When we read about Paul we notice that he had few large meetings, but he left behind churches that grew and matured. He was able to impart revelations that are still applicable today. There was something unusual in the ministry of Paul. When did he receive it? At conversion!

You may also realise that what you have in you today came when you were newly saved. You may not have understood it completely, but it was there. Every time God has given me 'new' revelation, when the Holy Spirit has illuminated something from the word of God that I hadn't seen before, it's not as though I was experiencing something completely new. Somehow, I could recognise it. It seems that everything God has told us to do has been lying waiting in a folder until God says it is time to take it out. I've always had it in me, because I've recognised it each time.

Israel is one such example which God spoke to us about very clearly some years ago. When I was a new Christian, God spoke to me about Israel for a while, but it never went any further than that at the time. When Word of Life started, people told me that we should start teaching about Israel. They asked and kept on asking! When I began to teach about Israel, they were overjoyed: 'Now we've got you where we want!' The truth is, I had it in me the whole time. The Holy Spirit told me not to be concerned about it for a while. At the end of the 70s and the beginning of the 80s, he told me not to take religious trips to Israel. 'Wait until I speak,' he said.

When God speaks, he takes out that folder and puts in something new. Although it's something new, you recognise it because God put it there in the beginning, when you were saved. This is even true if you were saved at a very young age and remember little of what happened then.

People will have problems for the rest of their lives if they don't accept what God has placed in them. From the start, God imparts the truth that Jesus is the healer, provider and baptiser in the Holy Spirit in each individual. Unfortunately, there are those who spend nearly their entire lives repressing and denying these truths. They end up with mental, emotional and other problems. Accept what is in your heart, and let God bring it to pass.

Your calling is your life!

I have declared to both Jews and Greeks that they must turn to God in repentance and have faith in our Lord Jesus. And now, compelled by the Spirit, I am going to Jerusalem, not knowing what will happen to me there. I only know that in every city the Holy Spirit warns me that prison and hardships are facing me. However, I consider my life worth nothing to me, if only I may finish the race and complete the task the Lord Jesus has given me – the task of testifying to the gospel of God's grace (Acts 20:21–24).

Does the Holy Spirit say things like that? Yes, the Holy Spirit's job is to lead you into all truth! This may sound very negative. However, Paul's chains kept him from being murdered by his fanatical opposition, and eventually took him to Rome at government expense! Everything wasn't negative, but the Holy Spirit was preparing Paul for circumstances that weren't completely positive. The Holy Spirit didn't say that a birthday party was waiting in Jerusalem. Paul got their attention when he arrived, but they were hiding daggers behind their backs. Paul said: 'But I consider my life to be of no value in itself. If God wants me to die in

Jerusalem, then I'll die there. I don't have an opinion about the matter. There's only one thing that I'm interested in, and that is to complete my race. I must do all that belongs to the office I've received from Jesus, to testify of God's gospel of grace. I don't live for myself, for my ministry, or for what people think I should do. If it's God's will that I should die, then I'm ready. However, if the devil wants to stop me from finishing my race, then I am not willing. I am not willing to satisfy the devil, only Jesus. I have only one race to run, and my life has no purpose outside my calling!'

Remember that you don't have a life outside your calling! Some people constantly swing back and forth with the world. They try to establish two lives: one in church and one at work, a religious life and a secular life. But if you try to walk on two roads simultaneously, you're sure to fall on one of them. There is only one life. Either you live for God or you live for the devil. You are either for God's calling or for the world. 'But a little sin won't hurt anything!' Wrong! Avoid all sin, because a 'dead' person never responds to anything from the world.

Of course, people will think that you are a fool. Do you imagine that the world is going to pin a medal on you for long and faithful service? Is the world going to fall at your feet and say: 'We knew you were noble, kind and loving'? If you think 'Eventually they are going to accept me,' then you're wrong. The world will never accept you. When you die, they might build a little monument to your memory, set up a statue or write on a plaque. That's what the world has always done. The world stones prophets, then decorates their graves.

As long as you live for God, you will meet resistance. It didn't take Paul long to get these results when he began to preach:

> Yet Saul grew more and more powerful and baffled the Jews living in Damascus by proving that Jesus is the Christ. After many days had gone by, the Jews conspired to kill him (Acts 9:22–23).

Were they just a little upset because they thought Paul was ruining their fun? No, they eventually decided to get rid of him. They were going to kill him! The devil saw right away what was going to happen.

A dedicated Christian is always a threat to the devil and his kingdom. You're going to upset him and he's going to persecute you. No wonder you always need to be strong in the Lord and in his mighty power!

6

The Apostle Proclaims the Full Counsel of God

Of the five ministry gifts, two are general in nature and three are specialised. The teacher, prophet and evangelist are specialised, while the pastor and apostle are general.

The pastor is the 'general practitioner' in the local church. He must proclaim all God's counsel, not one subject or single revelation.

The same is true of the apostle, except that he ministers to a larger area. Many different things are done while an apostle establishes a church. When he arrives in a new area, the apostle functions as an evangelist and leads people to salvation. He then functions as a teacher and instructor, helping them mature in the Lord. Eventually, he installs co-workers and leaders, and serves as their pastor. In addition, he prophesies and challenges them in the Holy Spirit.

The apostle has the well-being of the church very strongly upon his heart – both the universal church, which is the body of Christ, and the local church. He's involved with the individual believer as well as with the breadth and length, height and depth of all that God is doing. The apostle has an overview of all God's counsel. Paul says:

> For I have not hesitated to proclaim to you the whole will of God. Keep watch over yourselves and all the flock of which the Holy Spirit has

made you overseers. Be shepherds of the church of God, which he bought with his own blood. I know that after I leave, savage wolves will come in among you and will not spare the flock. Even from your own number men will arise and distort the truth in order to draw away disciples after them. So be on your guard! Remember that for three years I never stopped warning each of you night and day with tears. Now I commit you to God and to the word of his grace, which can build you up and give you an inheritance among all those who are sanctified. I have not coveted anyone's silver or gold or clothing (Acts 20:27–33).

Paul is saying that the church, which has been established, will be attacked. 'Wolves will come, but remember that I warned every one of you.' Elsewhere in the Bible we can see that Paul admonishes, encourages and corrects.

A leader must dare to confront

Admonishing or warning is something that has often been forgotten in the church. Leaders have been afraid to rub against people's flesh. They would rather 'stay friendly' with people with whom they barely agree, but who have never received the help they had a right to expect. What kind of church have they chosen? Did they only want to gather a random crowd and preach a lukewarm message that would satisfy the majority but not pierce their hearts and change their lives? If so, then they're not the servants of Jesus Christ that God intended!

You must dare to confront if you are a pastor, a spiritual leader or you function in other ministry gifts. And this is especially true for the apostle. God put the apostle on the front line to hit the devil hard! Apostles have the strength to hit hard! If God has put them on the front line, then you know the devil will try to tear them from this position. If God establishes a pastor in a church, then the devil will also try to break him down. The devil always tries to remove those God has put in a position of leadership and replace them with those who shouldn't be in positions of leadership.

Sometimes, people can be totally confused about leadership. Everyone wants to play leader and have something to say. They run around prophesying over each other like children playing a game. The church isn't a playground! God doesn't want it to be like this, but rather like the church in Colosse:

> For though I am absent from you in body, I am present with you in spirit and delight to see how orderly you are and how firm your faith in Christ is (Col 2:5).

The devil resists God-given, anointed leadership. He is terrified of established leadership because it creates an atmosphere of security, freedom, stability and maturity in the church. The devil wants a pack of crazy, howling dogs that go for each other's throats. He wants church members to be insecure, always running around behind each other's backs. But that's not what he's going to get!

Confront in love

We often think that we should be sweet and positive and never say anything to the people who really need correction. Paul was positive, but his warnings were very strong. We may have misunderstood this aspect of the apostolic ministry. It may seem hard, categorical and without love, but it isn't, even when someone like Paul scathingly confronts someone. In his letter to Timothy, he writes:

> Among them are Hymenaeus and Alexander, whom I have handed over to Satan to be taught not to blaspheme (1 Tim 1:20).

> Alexander the metalworker did me a great deal of harm. The Lord will repay him for what he has done (2 Tim 4:14).

We still recognise this Alexander two thousand years later. Paul publicly nailed him with such force that we still feel the effects today! Not many preachers have spoken like this from the pulpit, have they? Matthew 23 also describes the way Jesus spoke to the Pharisees. We're often afraid of this because it's too controversial. But we aren't called to be nice. We're called to be loving, and this is totally different. Love is always linked to truth.

People are sometimes afraid to say anything that might be interpreted as negative, because they've been taught to have a positive confession:

'If you walk there, you might fall in and drown!'

'No, forget it. I can't say that because it's too negative.' This is foolishness. Positive confession means speaking according to God's word and not wasting our time with negative gossip. If God's word says that we are to challenge, discipline and correct, then that's exactly what we should do. We often want to please people and be liked. This is not only awful but destructive. Paul says:

> You know we never used flattery, nor did we put on a mask to cover up greed – God is our witness (1 Thess 2:5).

This is vital, especially for individual churches. A pastor who looks happy and says, 'Hallelujah! You're the best congregation in the world!' may not have a problem gaining members. But if he never chastises, cleanses or challenges, he'll end up with a bunch of wild hyenas in his church. The pastor must watch over them!

Getting people saved is not enough. The newly saved need to grow in the Lord as well. If the Holy Spirit shows you something about a person, then you will need to confront them in love. Clearly communicate what God is saying to you: 'Something is wrong here, and you need to change your attitude.' If they get angry with you, then let them get angry! Don't worry about creating divisions. Some division is good! The word, which is the sword of the Spirit, divides between spirit and soul. Those thoughts that are soulish in nature, and not from heaven, need to be dealt with and removed. Otherwise, the devil will use these thoughts to weaken and destroy the church and prevent revival.

These areas must be dealt with! The apostle and prophet see it, as should the pastor. The evangelist should open his eyes and see it as well. The teacher cannot hide behind his own concerns and ignore it either. The ministry gifts must challenge, watch, encourage, strengthen and stabilise the church. Truth needs to be faced. They need to discern what is correct doctrine, and the difference between order and disorder. Otherwise, the body of Christ will never be strong, pure and filled with the glory of the Lord!

Paul's letters – doctrine and exhortation

Nurturing a church is an ongoing process. New people always come, and they always bring new ideas with them. They may be shocked to find they have to lay aside their own ambitions to work on something new, or in a way they aren't accustomed to. They may have been used to receiving a certain amount of attention, and suddenly everything is different. Their lives are being shaken: 'I feel threatened!' Hallelujah, it's about time! Everything that isn't of God needs to be pulled up by the roots. This weeding out shouldn't take all our time, but it should be done when necessary.

Paul's letters to the churches are divided into doctrine and exhortation. He challenged his readers at length and went into great detail as well: how they should dress, how they should work, how they should treat people of the opposite sex. He spoke about their marriages and their relationship to authority. Paul didn't just teach about healing. He covered everything.

Some are disturbed by what Paul wrote concerning marriage in Ephesians 5. These people aren't carnal unbelievers, but people who love speaking in tongues and praying for the sick. They fail to see that 1 Corinthians 12 and Ephesians 5 are equally anointed of the Holy Spirit! Paul says that he hasn't restrained himself from proclaiming all God's counsel.

The church must meet every need

God's end-time church will be strong in every area, meeting every human need. The church will not only be strong in the areas of healing and salvation but have apostolic characteristics, dealing with every aspect of a person's life.

When the apostolic anointing enters a church, it creates a spearhead and a breadth that turns the church into a spiritual giant! This won't happen overnight; it takes years to develop completely. But the result will be dynamic churches that meet every kind of need. They will meet charity needs as well as local and foreign needs. They will supply spiritual leadership in areas that the devil has stolen, and reclaim them for Jesus. Jesus wants to place every area of human life in subjection to him. Certain areas remain under the devil's control. He has the upper hand and laughs at the church, just as Goliath ridiculed the children of Israel, and left them scared and trembling. But God will change all of this! The devil has made the church appear ridiculous, backwards and strange, making it a laughing stock for everyone. The world will always laugh, for what the church does is often foolishness in its eyes. But God's word is relevant to every aspect of life: finances, business, the media, family life, sports, culture, the arts, politics, education, health care and charity. God has something to say about everything! The pattern is in the church!

Sometimes, we have become so 'over-spiritual' that we lose interest in our influence on society. In turn, we've delegated this responsibility to backslidden Christians and unbelievers, thereby creating an anti-Christian environment. But God wants to restore society! He wants to show, through the church, how everything can flow from a source of purity, holiness and righteousness. God can meet all these needs through the local church, which is based on the heavenly blueprint.

Therefore, the church needs to receive this through accepting the apostolic and prophetic ministries, which have a greater dimension than the other gifts. The apostle and prophet strengthen the local churches, bringing growth, breakthrough and victory!

7

The Apostle Is Called to the World

An apostle's calling is strong! Paul was totally preoccupied with the fact that Jesus had called him. He had no alternative!

> For this purpose I was appointed a herald and an apostle – I am telling the truth, I am not lying – and a teacher of the true faith to the Gentiles (1 Tim 2:7).

In other words, an apostle is both preacher and teacher, as was Paul.

A preacher can be an evangelist or a pastor. The Greek word for 'preach' means to proclaim. Everyone can preach or proclaim. In the past, heralds entered a city and proclaimed: 'The King is coming! The King is coming!' They sounded a trumpet and read a message from the king: 'This is the law from now on!'

A teacher instructs, explains and helps people understand. Paul also said that he was a teacher in his apostolic ministry. He taught about truth, faith and 'the word of faith, which we are proclaiming' (Rom 10:8). Faith is what you and I live by, for the just shall live by faith.

Sometimes, preachers who are capable and wonderful instructors of faith, become frightened when it comes to proclaiming the truth. We must lay a foundation by teaching faith, because every individual member needs to believe totally in God's word. But

God also wants to reveal truth. Truth is what the Holy Spirit says about different circumstances. There is truth about the future: when the Holy Spirit reveals truth about you, your family, your church and the city in which you live. He does it to build you up, strengthen you and make you free.

Nothing can stop the truth when it is proclaimed with a prophetic anointing. Truth causes change and sets people free.

Let the Holy Spirit set you apart

Paul was called to the nations. Therefore, he could never be satisfied to sit in Damascus and hold Bible studies for fifty years! Something else drew him. He felt he had to leave Damascus. Eventually, he also left Antioch, led by the Holy Spirit.

The Holy Spirit set Paul apart in the church at Antioch to prepare him for the apostolic ministry (Acts 13:1–3). Remember that your time will come as well! You may have been called, but perhaps you're starting to wonder about it. You may even be getting impatient. You will never need to manipulate or push ahead of anyone else. God has his time for you. If you serve the Most High, the Holy Spirit will show you when to begin the task God has given you. It's much better to be set apart by the Holy Spirit than by men. In Antioch, people fasted and prayed, praised God, laid hands on Paul, set him apart and prophesied over him. Yet he says in his letter to the Galatians: 'Paul, an apostle – sent not from men nor by man' (Gal 1:1). The book of Acts doesn't even mention the names of the people who laid hands on Paul and prophesied. We don't need to know the details, just what the Holy Spirit is saying.

The TV screen is today's town square

Paul was set apart and began his ministry with a deep longing to reach new areas for the Lord. It's characteristic of the apostolic anointing and ministry to move on as soon as an area has been taken and added to the kingdom of Jesus Christ. The area might be geographical or spiritual, such as, 'I need more spiritual insight in this area of the Christian life!' Another may relate to an area of interest, since God is concerned with every area of life. 'The gospel must be heard in every school, and every preschooler needs to hear it as well. Then of course, we need to get on television!'

When Paul entered a city, he would head for the town square, since that was where the people were. Today, few people gather in the town square, unless it's Saturday and a market is there. If you want to find out where the people are, you'll have to look in front of their televisions. If you want to reach them, then you'll have to knock on their TV screens!

Since Word of Life began in 1983, we have tried to break our government's monopoly over radio and television. Recently, the monopoly has been broken. This opens the way for a lot of rubbish, but much good can now be done as well. State-controlled television that won't broadcast revival Christianity isn't worth having anyway! Unfortunately, our television screens broadcast a so-called Christianity that is not just a poor imitation of the real thing, but almost another religion! You can talk about God, but what god are you talking about? You can talk about Jesus, but which Jesus? You can talk about the cross, but what happened there? You can talk about salvation, but what does being saved really mean? You can talk about life in God and about being born again, but what does that mean? There are people who use the same words that you and I do, but they mean something totally different.

At times, the message has been presented by people who have never been born again. Others may have been saved, but have become deceived and fallen into 'doctrines of devils', eventually falling away from God. 'Having a form of godliness but denying its power' (2 Tim 3:5). Many such people are in both our religious and secular institutions. They have access to the national radio and television, but the gospel they preach isn't from the Bible. They alter the gospel, and another spirit is behind much of what they do.

The Bible speaks about people pressing in on Jesus to hear the word of God, and to be healed from their diseases (Lk 5:1). Ask yourself where in your country, or the world for that matter, people eagerly press in to hear the gospel and be healed. People go where Jesus is. Any message can be spread through TV, universities, and theological institutions. Look at the local church! Are there any people there? No. Why not? Because the message preached lacks the power of attraction from God. The gospel is the power of God to salvation. If the gospel isn't preached, then there's no power. God wants this to stop. People have the right to hear from heaven.

Apostolic ministries can vary

Although the apostle is always on the move towards new territory, he is not restless. He may be called to the world, but as we see with Paul, he didn't run around aimlessly. He was carefully led by the Holy Spirit.

The Bible tells us about Paul's desire and attempt to enter Asia, but the Holy Spirit wouldn't allow it. Instead he received a revelation, a vision in a dream of a man from Macedonia. God opened the door to an entire continent and gave him the key to Europe. Philippi wasn't just a new city for Paul, it was a new continent! The gospel entered Europe with consequences that would affect world history.

It's important to avoid stereotypes. You may see the apostle as a missionary who travels around to start churches, but this isn't the entire picture. The apostle can function in a variety of ways. Many of the first apostles didn't travel much in the beginning. Peter stayed close to Jerusalem, even if he occasionally took an odd trip within the immediate area. On the other hand, when Paul received his calling, he also received the world as his territory. Apostolic ministry can be shown in different ways. Some have a strong emphasis on international work, while others may be called to a special country or region.

You must understand the apostolic ministry

There are two reasons why you need to understand how the apostolic ministry functions. First, we cannot always be certain that someone is an apostle simply because they say that they are. They may have started a work somewhere and preached in the area around their home, but that doesn't automatically make them apostles. Every believer should take initiatives, but that doesn't make us all apostles.

You never need to run around and tell people what you are. They'll know by the fruit. Signs speak for themselves. If you are a prophet or function in a prophetic way, then what you say will happen. Look at Samuel – not a word that he spoke fell aimlessly to the ground. All that he said came to pass. Through this, all Israel understood that Samuel was entrusted with the word of the Lord. This was a sign of Samuel's prophetic ministry. When he said something would happen, it did!

The other reason you need to understand the apostolic ministry is to be free from fear when an apostle comes. In the past, the apostle has functioned in unusual ways. Here in Sweden, we've had military, political and social disarmament. Worse yet, in many areas we have even had total spiritual disarmament. This is terrible, but God has an answer: 'But where sin increased, grace increased all the more' (Rom 5:20). God is in the process of restoring Sweden. We believe in revival Christianity, not cultural Christianity! We believe in the full gospel. The Holy Spirit will affect this country in a way that will make an impact! As Acts 26:26 says, 'since this thing was not done in a corner' (NKJV).

Today, Jesus is not just walking through the countryside, but through the cities. Paul didn't just preach in mountain villages or small settlements in the country. He hit the greatest cities of his time with full force: Jerusalem, Damascus, Antioch, Ephesus, Corinth and Rome. The same thing is going to happen today. God wants to hit our greatest cities with his Holy Spirit. There is a great harvest in the cities today!

Give the apostle the freedom to work

The choices an apostle makes affect the future as well as the present. His method of working, his daily routine and relationships are vital. Therefore, the enemy attacks the apostle's ministry by weighing him down with unnecessary burdens. If the apostle loses perspective, he won't be able to finish his race.

This is generally true for all of the ministry gifts. As a believer and member of a local church, you don't have the right to concern your pastor, teacher or prophet with what you think they should do. I know pastors who were asked by members of their church to come over and change their tyres. You can do this, but Jesus didn't say: 'Go ye into all the world and change tyres!' or, 'Go ye into all the world and be buried by a stack of paperwork in your office!' That's why you should always pray that your pastor or leader is free to minister as God intends. Pray that they will be able to do what they are called to do. They should not be burdened with all the little things that so many others could do instead, and do better.

Paul had a tremendous need for this freedom, because he had a travelling ministry. He wasn't just called to Antioch, but to all the Gentiles. The apostle isn't content with one area, even if like Paul he finds himself in a place for a longer period doing foundational work before he moves on. Paul had the entire world as his mission field!

8

Training Disciples and Teams

A vital area of the apostle's ministry is his ability to train disciples and develop support teams. The apostle does this because he can see further than a single meeting, prophetic message or anointing and momentary victory.

I have described the apostle as God's architect, who has received a blueprint from heaven. An architect, or master builder, knows that you can't build a house in five minutes. He doesn't get depressed when he comes to a construction site and finds it filled with clay, sand and stone. He can see what it will look like, when others only see a boring and ugly site. If you judge a minister by one meeting, or a church after one week, then it shows that you can't see very far ahead. God wants you to see further.

An apostle isn't satisfied to toss out a net, catch fish, and throw them on the beach and say: 'Isn't it fantastic! What a great catch!' The work has only just started! The fish need to be sorted, cleaned and prepared before they can be eaten. Fame doesn't begin here, but rather work and preparation!

The preparation period is the most important period of your life. Don't miss it! The devil wants to force you out before you're ready, and make you do things now, instead of waiting until you're mature and prepared. God has a plan for everyone's life, and everyone needs to be trained and developed. Think about Jesus: he had thirty years of preparation, followed by three and a half years of effective ministry that changed the world. The Holy Spirit also took time to prepare Paul for his calling. He was under training in Antioch until the Holy Spirit spoke to the leaders of the church. He was sent to fulfil his calling when he was prepared.

Timothy became Paul's disciple, 'handpicked' while he was out preaching (Acts 16:1–5). 'You're going to start travelling with me,' Paul said, 'because God has a plan for your life and you need to be trained and developed.'

Iron sharpens iron

No man is an island. Everyone has a time in which they are raised, trained and developed. It's a time when people rub against each other in a process that perfects. 'As iron sharpens iron, so one man sharpens another' (Prov 27:17). If you want to be something for God, then you're going to be admonished by him. Some people get so upset when they're always 'rubbed up the wrong way'. John Osteen said a few years ago, 'If the cat doesn't like being rubbed up the wrong way, then the cat needs to turn around!'

When I was newly saved, I had the privilege of staying with a family of wonderful Christians. The father in the house began to train me, almost against my will. One day when I came home from the university, he was waiting for me by the front gate.

'Do you see anything special about this gate?' he asked after exchanging greetings.

'No,' I answered. Then we walked down the path.

'Do you see anything special about the flower bed?' he asked.

'Ah, they're flowers, aren't they?' I answered.

We walked to the steps where we could see a bag of rubbish.

'Do you see anything special here?'

'Well, there's a bag of rubbish here.'

We went on into the kitchen.

'Do you see anything here?' he wondered.

'Dishes,' I said.

'So,' he said at last, 'we have just taken a tour around the house and you've seen all these things. What did you think when you saw them?' I started to chafe a bit inside. He took me outside again.

'This is a gate,' he said. 'It needs painting. It doesn't need to be prophesied over, but painted. Here is the flower bed that needs to be weeded. I've noticed that you've walked past this bag of rubbish every day without reacting at all. It should be taken to the dustbin. These are your dishes. You took off this morning to do what you wanted, and left them. That's all you think about,' he said, 'you and yourself!'

I was ashamed to tears, because he was completely right. Do you know what he was doing? He was training me in a right spirit.

The apostle trains and teaches his disciples

An apostle teaches and trains his disciples. This is what Paul said to Timothy:

> You then, my son, be strong in the grace that is in Christ Jesus. And the things you have heard me say in the presence of many witnesses entrust to reliable men who will also be qualified to teach others (2 Tim 2:1–2).

Paul was unbelievably bold when he spoke of himself as an example. He often said, 'Do as I do, think as I think, and everything will be fine.' There aren't many preachers who would stand up and say that! Apparently, Christianity was somewhat different in those days from what it is in many churches today.

In Paul's day, it was normal for a master to train and teach apprentices. The same was true of disciples. It wasn't an extreme form of leadership, where the disciple had to ask his spiritual leader for advice about every detail of his life, and where the leader wasn't sure of an answer until he had heard from heaven. Instead, there was an atmosphere of training and helping around the master. The same atmosphere is around the apostle, and eventually, it will be transferred to the local church.

> And the things you have heard me say . . . entrust to reliable men who will also be qualified to teach others (2 Tim 2:2).

This is an example of how the message is passed on through four generations: from Paul to Timothy, on to 'faithful men' and from them to others. The apostle always keeps the future in mind. 'What I have, you shall have, and when you've received it, give it to someone else who can pass it on to others.'

Paul worked in a team

Training is linked with obedience. When you give yourself to Jesus Christ, you also give yourself to the Holy Spirit who makes you aware of your weak points, and helps you deal with them.

This shaping of character is part of the apostle's ministry. Paul used a large portion of his letters to challenge his readers in practical areas. You can have all the anointing in the world, but God knows that if your character hasn't been trained and put in subjection to Christ, then your areas of weakness will surface in times of stress and conflict. Without training, you won't pass the tests.

You'll notice two interesting things about Paul in the book of Acts. One is that he speaks very freely about himself, and the other is that he is always surrounded by co-workers. He always has a team with him.

> While they were worshipping the Lord and fasting, the Holy Spirit said, 'Set apart for me Barnabas and Saul for the work to which I have called them.' So after they had fasted and prayed, they placed their hands on them and sent them off (Acts 13:2–3).

Here we read about an entire team, and not just a lone preacher. Look at Paul! He still hasn't finished his training. He has Barnabas to help and exhort him. Soon, we no longer read 'Barnabas and Paul' but 'Paul and Barnabas'. The master is now finished with his disciple. The disciple has surpassed his master, but Barnabas isn't irritated, angry or jealous. Barnabas is happy to have helped Paul. He introduced Paul to the apostles, put him in the right place, spent time with him in the church and then participated in sending him out. When Paul moves on, he is never alone. There are always people around him.

I strongly believe that an individual should take the initiative and that a believer should be led by the Holy Spirit. I don't agree with a kind of spiritualised socialistic collectivism in charismatic clothing! God leads every individual, but there is a limit. We are part of a bigger picture. Didn't Jesus send out his disciples two by two?

The apostle thinks beyond a single campaign

They preached the good news in that city and won a large number of disciples. Then they returned to Lystra, Iconium and Antioch, strengthening the disciples and encouraging them to remain true to the faith. 'We must go through many hardships to enter the kingdom of God,' they said. Paul and Barnabas appointed elders for them in each church and, with prayer and fasting, committed them to the Lord, in whom they had put their trust (Acts 14:21–23).

The team comes to Lystra, Iconium, and Antioch, and people in all these places are saved. They then travel on. It doesn't take long until Paul is back again. Why? Because he thinks beyond a single campaign. He checks on those who were not just saved, but became disciples. In the Bible, a person does not make a decision to be saved, but to be a disciple. Disciples give their lives to Jesus.

Paul spent time with those who had become disciples. He strengthened them, spoke to them and imparted something to them. He trained them as disciples, and gave them stability. He told them to stand fast in the faith. He admonished them and gave them a realistic picture of what it meant to be saved. He gave them the full gospel, with power, victory and blessing from heaven, but he also made it clear that the Christian life wasn't a bed of roses. 'You'll be attacked and experience affliction, but if you stand fast you'll be cared for in a wonderful way!'

The elders in the church weren't chosen immediately, only when the time was right. It was the responsibility of Paul and Barnabas as ministers to appoint them. They didn't ask who wanted to be an elder! They checked who would be faithful and continue with the Lord. Then Paul and Barnabas went on their way. Together, they formed a small team, which would steadily increase.

Proper order in the team

Paul and his companions travelled throughout the region of Phrygia and Galatia, having been kept by the Holy Spirit from preaching the word in the province of Asia. When they came to the border of Mysia, they tried to enter Bithynia, but the Spirit of Jesus would not allow them to. So they passed by Mysia and went down to Troas. During the night Paul had a vision of a man of Macedonia standing and begging him, 'Come over to Macedonia and help us.' After Paul had seen the vision, we got ready at once to leave for Macedonia, concluding that God had called us to preach the gospel to them (Acts 16:6–10).

There is no doubt about the identity of the leader of this team. When reading the letters, you may notice that they state 'Paul and Timothy' or 'Paul and Silvanus'. Paul had a group around him, and the group had an internal order. Everyone knew who was who. They worked together and had tremendous power!

In many churches there is a collectivist stream that does not allow anyone to be anything special. If one is an elder, then all are to be elders. If one is a pastor, then all are to be pastors and so on. Everyone has to be at the same level. How foolish! However, neither is it right to push things to the extreme, to a kind of ultra-individualism, where only one person is important and the rest are to sit passively by.

Paul's apostolic team demonstrated good order. One can easily distinguish Paul from the others, but the others can also be distinguished. We read that God spoke to Paul, but Luke comments by saying, 'Then we understood that we were called.' He didn't say, 'Paul is called, so we'd better join him if we're going to have any fun!' Luke says instead, 'We are called.'

The Holy Spirit brings ministries together

He was accompanied by Sopater son of Pyrrhus from Berea, Aristarchus and Secundus from Thessalonica, Gaius from Derbe, Timothy also, and Tychicus and Trophimus from the province of Asia (Acts 20:4).

This was Paul's team. He chose people from the churches he helped to start. He took them with him, taught, strengthened and admonished them. They were his co-workers.

In the future, we will no longer work alone, because the Holy Spirit will join together ministers, those who are mature with those who are being developed. It will happen in the way the Holy Spirit wants. These will not be small cliques, but servants joined as a mighty hammer of God that breaks through in cities and nations. No matter how strong and anointed they are, individual ministers will learn to co-operate with each other. It's not a matter of losing one's identity, but rather of finding one's place.

Paul trained and influenced others to develop and continue the work he had begun. They heard his teaching, saw his example, watched what he did and saw God's hand on his life. When they were mature, he sent them out into God's service.

> The reason I left you in Crete was that you might straighten out what was left unfinished and appoint elders in every town, as I directed you (Tit 1:5).

Paul went on his way as the Holy Spirit led. But there were still things to do, so Titus remained.

9

The Church – the Base for Every Ministry

Our personal faith must also be lived publically through the local church. I believe that God's perception of the local church differs from the traditional idea, so you must be prepared for a change.

The apostle Paul is an example for every Christian, because his life was spent in fellowship with a local church. Paul travelled extensively and had a strong and independent ministry, yet he always tied everything to the church at Antioch. He was sent out and supported by the church. After his travels, he returned to the church to share his experiences. Until he was detained in Rome, this church was Paul's base.

At times, the local church has controlled and imprisoned ministry gifts. This isn't God's will! Every ministry needs to relate to a local church, no matter how strong, powerful and anointed it may be or how many manifestations take place. God has given a vision, a mission to the local church. You may feel that your own vision will die when you submit to the vision of a local church, but this isn't necessarily true. It's possible for a strong and anointed ministry to find rest and security in a relationship to the local church, and still fulfil God's calling. You don't need to come into conflict with the vision God has laid upon the church. Conflicts have nothing to do with the vision one has. Conflicts arise through the condition of the heart.

75

Submission doesn't mean a lack of freedom. This is extremely important, even for the apostolic ministry. Paul didn't have this problem. He came to Antioch, left and travelled most of the time. There is not one negative word about his home church in any of his letters, because there was a right attitude and true relationship between them. Paul wasn't held captive by a local church. He not only had fellowship with a local church, but he was also loyal to it.

Paul never assumed he had authority over the churches across the Roman Empire. Yet his authority was without question in the churches he or his disciples established. They had a special relationship with each other. This is why he says to the Corinthians,

> Even though you have ten thousand guardians in Christ, you do not have many fathers, for in Christ Jesus I became your father through the gospel (1 Cor 4:15).

Paul had a special relationship with this church. How different to those who call themselves apostles, travelling from church to church, demanding submission and obedience!

All of the ministry gifts and gifts of the Spirit will be represented in apostolic churches. Here, the ministry gifts will be constantly trained and developed, while strong apostolic teams are sent out. Strong ministers will have the freedom to work. We are going to see churches with powerful missions work and witness believers going out and influencing society.

Don't be afraid to let other ministries in!

The five ministry gifts must have a good relationship with different churches. The pastor is the only stationary ministry gift, but even he can visit other churches. The pastor of a church needs to maintain a relationship to the teacher, prophet, evangelist and apostle. He should never close the door to them or be afraid of them. Instead, he needs to be aware of what they have to give and be prepared to receive it, because it will enrich the church. The pastor shouldn't be nervous and think that he can do it all himself.

If you are a pastor, don't be afraid to let someone in. Sheep follow their shepherd, even if a minister who is 'better' or more anointed than you should come. If the shepherd is secure with his anointing, and keeps a relaxed attitude towards his congregation and other ministers, then they will enrich, strengthen and stabilise the church. They won't take anything away from it.

The shepherd's heart reaches out to his sheep. He has a heart for the people and gladly overlooks mistakes and sins. Even if a brother has fallen twenty times, the pastor will start over from the beginning: 'It's okay, we'll pray for you. Don't give up, everything will work out.' The shepherd's heart is filled to overflowing, but he must not neglect two important areas. A pastor may be satisfied to get people saved, but they also need to be sanctified and cleansed. A pastor can also compromise regarding the different things God is doing through the church, and in relation to what the Holy Spirit is saying. The pastor is primarily concerned with doing his own job.

The apostle stands guard over doctrine

The ministry of the evangelist is vital for the body of Christ. However, the methods the evangelist uses will change and we must be prepared for this. The evangelist himself must also be prepared for change as he will no longer use the methods of the 30s, 50s and 60s!

The evangelist hasn't always been blessed with discernment. Above all else, his heart is for the lost, the world and the heathen. One might hear an evangelist say, 'I don't care about the various doctrines. I just preach Jesus.' That's the evangelist! 'Amen,' you might say, thinking that doctrine isn't worth worrying about. If so, then you've been deceived. Try to preach Jesus without preaching doctrine! When you come to heaven and meet Paul, he's going to ask you a few things. 'I just preached Jesus,' you may say. Yes, we preach Jesus, but we also preach the revelation Jesus has given us in his word about the church, doctrine, life, morality, power and order.

In this regard, the apostle is different. He has the church and its development strongly upon his heart, as well as doctrine. The apostle watches over church doctrine. Paul speaks about this in Galatians:

> I am astonished that you are so quickly deserting the one who called you by the grace of Christ and are turning to a different gospel . . . I did not receive it from any man, nor was I taught it; rather, I received it by revelation from Jesus Christ (Gal 1:6, 12).

Do you know what this means? Guard doctrine and establish the gospel!

No ordinary unity

The evangelist has a wonderful heart. He has a spiritual personality that attracts people. He preaches the gospel strongly and clearly, with a mighty anointing. He can also teach, but that's not primarily his responsibility.

I don't believe that God has given the evangelist the task of uniting the body of Christ. Every ministry contributes to the establishment of unity. But one ministry gift achieves this in a unique way. The apostle has the body of Christ strongest on his heart!

The evangelist may say, 'Let's put aside our differences about baptism and just preach Jesus.' This can be accepted for the duration of a campaign or something similar, but you cannot build lasting unity like this. Of course, it's wonderful when several churches unite to do something, but this kind of unity seldom lasts. Sometimes, it results in chaos.

Limits need to be set, and the prophet and the apostle do this, although they have different ministries. Their ministries need to be accepted because they can see where the body of Christ is heading, and clearly speak about doctrine, order and direction. Otherwise, we'll end up with a muddled fellowship that is not of the Holy Spirit, and impossible to maintain.

Stronger ministries are needed for follow-up

Philip went down to a city in Samaria and proclaimed the Christ there. When the crowds heard Philip and saw the miraculous signs he did, they all paid close attention to what he said. With shrieks, evil spirits came out of many, and many paralytics and cripples were healed. So there was great joy in that city (Acts 8: 5–8).

Here we see Philip the evangelist at work. He is incredibly powerful. Philip was linked to the church in Jerusalem, but had a great deal of freedom out in the harvest fields.

In the rest of the chapter, we see something interesting and somewhat unusual compared to the way follow-up is normally handled. When Philip finished his work people started to listen and to respect his message. Then the apostles came. The weaker ministers didn't come for the follow-up phase; the stronger did! I'm not using the term 'stronger' to put the others down. Philip didn't look for someone with nothing else to do and send him to Samaria to encourage the believers! Stronger ministries were sent there instead, so the harvest wouldn't be lost. When the campaign was over, the real work began.

If you announce figures after a campaign, make sure you tell the truth and not how many hands were raised at the invitation or how many happened to be at the meeting. It's more fun to say, 'Ten thousand people came to the meeting!' than to say, 'Five people were saved.' Let's talk about disciples. How many remained?

'But no one will give money to support five people!'

Then I suggest that you start having faith in God.

'Yes, but then I won't get any money.'

If all that matters is money, then you'd better become a banker instead!

'If people give money then I should give them exciting reports.'

No, not if you are in fellowship with a church that believes in what you're doing.

The church is vital for lasting fruit

Imagine this: the church is one hundred per cent with you before you arrive in a city, while you are there and after you leave. That's what God wants. He has placed the ministry gifts in the local church to continue the work of the Holy Spirit in that place.

Therefore, there's a strength and a stability in the work, and lasting fruit. There are no large campaigns where disciples are hard to find after a while. This is what God wants, but we have seldom achieved it.

Recently, I spoke about follow-up with an evangelist who is mightily used of God. He said: 'This is where we feel guilty. It's hard to have an effective follow-up work.' I believe that a strong local church is one solution to the problem!

Listen to your teachers

God wants you to see the church as a wonderful, steadily growing garden in which you are a part of the work. In this garden, you can do what Jesus has called you to do. You'll be trained, taught and involved.

> Obey your leaders and submit to their authority. They keep watch over you as men who must give an account. Obey them so that their work will be a joy, not a burden, for that would be of no advantage to you. Pray for us. We are sure that we have a clear conscience and desire to live honourably in every way (Heb 13:17–18).

God has placed leaders and teachers in the church. They are to work from the church and they will work with you! They are anointed to watch over your soul – your mind and thoughts. No one can force himself into another person's spirit, because the spirit only has room for Jesus and you. Yet so much is happening in your soul. We need to be trained in right understanding, to overcome our preconceptions and fleshly thoughts. Not accepting correction or advice from another is proof of rebellion. So listen to your teachers, put your own ideas on a back burner and stop being stubborn!

Once, someone came to me and wanted to ask me something since I was 'his shepherd'. When I heard him say that, I thought: 'Aha, it's going to be interesting to see whether I really am his shepherd.'

He asked whether I thought he should do this or that. I answered, 'You not only should do this, but must do it this way!'

A pastor can't know everything in every situation, but I felt very strongly in this case that a certain thing was right and the other was wrong. (There is an anointing for this as well. We cannot live by opinions alone.)

'Yes,' said the person in question, 'but I've already decided to do something else instead!'

'Why did you ask me then?' I wondered.

'Well, I just wanted to check it out with someone, that's all.'

'But you've already decided. You didn't want to check things out with someone. You wanted someone to say: "Thus says the Lord: Amen to your ideas!" What if you're wrong?'

'But I am the one who decides anyway.'

'No, Jesus decides.'

'Yes, Jesus decides, of course. Not you!'

'I'm your shepherd,' I said to this person who was a little shocked. 'You're acting as your own shepherd. If you really thought that I was your shepherd, then you would listen to what I had to say.'

'Yes, but you're not always right.'

'I'm not always wrong either! If you say you want my advice, don't just expect advice from an ordinary person. Open your heart for the pastor's anointing. You open your heart so that the Holy Spirit can say something you hadn't thought of yourself.'

You can of course live your life as I live mine, but the Bible says that the shepherd watches over the souls of the flock. This person did exactly what he wanted anyway. He has, of course, every right to do so, as well as the right to suffer the consequences of his actions. No one is forced to do anything. People do what they want anyway!

You have a ministry and a calling in the church

Paul says, 'Obey your leaders and submit to their authority. They keep watch over you as men who must give an account' (Heb 13:17). Nor should you go to the other extreme and disappear into some sort of 'collective anonymity'. You are an individual. God has a place and a way for you which goes through the church. You aren't a number in the membership roll that tithes. You are an individual with a ministry and a calling in the church.

There is so much potential in the local church. Imagine a church of a few thousand people whose members aren't just members, but true disciples. This is how God sees the local church. There are teams of ministry gifts with all the gifts represented. There is order and someone who leads the work. There is a vision, but also a sensitivity in the Holy Spirit for every individual member to find his place. When this is accomplished, then everyone will be able to come into the creativity that scares the devil to death.

This is the kind of church we want! Churches that evangelise, train, exercise spiritual authority, accept spirit responsibility, rule in the spiritual realm and prophesy to authorities. These churches provide the freedom for strong gifts to function, have active missions programmes, and send out strong apostolic teams. These churches will reach the ends of the earth!

10

Resistance and Persecution

The beginning of the church age was fantastic. Yet it is just a pale reflection of God's end-time church. The final phase of the church's revelation and mission will be completed before Jesus returns. The ministry gifts will be in operation and the people will be prepared. Order is necessary for the glory to come. This means that our attitudes and relationships also need to be in order. We are going to see people with strong ministries, even stronger than Paul's. I am positive that the glory of the Lord is going to be incredibly strong upon the church in the Last Days:

> 'Arise, shine, for your light has come, and the glory of the Lord rises upon you. See, darkness covers the earth and thick darkness is over the peoples, but the Lord rises upon you and his glory appears over you' (Is 60:1–2).

Although we know that this refers to Israel, we can also apply it to the church. God is preparing us for the Last Days, so that we can function strongly. All ministries, all gifts, and all the glory will be restored and increased. God wants every area to develop so that the church will be preserved and endure.

Revival, glory, church growth and expansion are wonderful. This is the normal life for a Christian and it is planted deep in the heart of every believer. Unfortunately, we don't often understand the atmosphere in which all of this will occur. God will perform his work, but he will be using tough times to do it. God doesn't send the difficult times – the devil does – but God will take advantage of the situation.

A warlike atmosphere

Jesus says,

> And this gospel of the kingdom will be preached in the whole world as a testimony to all nations, and then the end will come (Matt 24:14).

What will the circumstances be like when this preaching of the gospel takes place? An atmosphere of deception. 'Watch out that no one deceives you' (Matt 24:4). There will also be wars and rumours of war. We must not lose our presence of mind (v 6). Nation will rise against nation, and there will be famine and earthquakes. Believers will be at the mercy of others and be killed.

> Then you will be handed over to be persecuted and put to death, and you will be hated by all nations because of me (v 9).

In the Last Days, many will be betrayed.

> At that time many will turn away from the faith and will betray and hate each other, and many false prophets will appear and deceive many people (Matt 24:10–11).

Lawlessness will reign and love will grow cold for most. This is the atmosphere in which the gospel of the kingdom will be preached to all nations! It won't be the best of times, but you'll make it, if you are prepared.

Because of this, God is preparing a certain kind of believer. A normal believer! He will be Spirit filled, tongues speaking and aware of his calling. Furthermore, he'll be able to handle the pressure! This is one of the most important things the Holy Spirit is doing today. Do you want spiritual power to flood into your life? Then renew your mind, turn away from sin, commit yourself wholeheartedly, get trained and purified and come into your calling, full of the fear of God. When the thunder starts, and explosions surround you, then you will shout, 'Praise the name of the Lord, it's starting to be normal!'

Paul was prepared

Our flesh doesn't enjoy these circumstances. We want peace and quiet. We want everyone to love us. Our circumstances won't be idyllic; they will be like it was in the book of Acts. The romantic side of revival is only half the truth.

Now we shouldn't go into our room, close the door and say: 'I don't want any part of this. Jesus is going to come and take me out of all this misery.' Don't be so sure! Jesus didn't come and take Paul out of his misery. He got saved, started preaching and soon after they wanted to kill him. That was the atmosphere he worked in. Encouraging beginning, wasn't it?

Paul came up against strong resistance and suffered constant attacks against his life and ministry, all because of the resounding revival that resulted from his ministry. As his execution approached, he could say: 'I have kept the faith, I've fought, I've run my race, I've finished my course, I've done what I was supposed to do and now there's just a quick chop left until I'm in heaven!'

Paul had an entirely different view of life than many Christians do. That's because he was prepared. He was successful because he was used to tough times. There was something in him that never gave up. He never started to slow down and plan for his retirement. He kept on fighting. He did what he was supposed to in spite of everything that came against him.

Have favour with God – not with the world

God's glory increases through difficult situations! Once we realise this we will neither be afraid of attacks nor try to theologically deny their existence. We'll begin to prepare for them instead. We'll start believing God for the victory. The circumstances will no longer hurt us, and we'll see that the situation wasn't worth worrying about. We will come through it all and the salvation of thousands will be the result.

One of the first things Jesus said to Paul was that he would suffer. He said, 'My grace is sufficient for you. You have a task that will not only affect the people in your immediate surroundings, but will also touch the lives of people for centuries. Therefore, I'll protect you and take you through it all. Nevertheless, you must understand that these things will happen. Don't be afraid, nervous or depressed. Don't think that you've made some mistake or that something is wrong with you. The anointing over you will stir up the opposition, but I'll protect you, keep you and complete all that I will do through you.'

There is no reason to preach persecution, but the backslidden church has misunderstood resistance for a long time. It hasn't dared to confront because it fears persecution, loneliness and isolation. The backslidden church has fawned over the world to the point of losing its savour! It's better to have favour with God than with the world. Grace before God and man will be found when we serve God. God has called you to the lost, and he will make sure that you reach them. But there will always be those who don't like what you are doing.

Be radical and be respected

We need to understand what is really happening. When the enemy reacts and gets angry, it just means that the kingdom of God is advancing! Many people have problems since they've been falsely taught to stay on good terms with everyone and everything. 'If it is possible, as far as it depends on you, live at peace with everyone' (Rom 12:18). Our attitude should be one of peace, love and blessing. However, you'll never have peace with the devil. Jesus said,

> 'Woe to you when all men speak well of you, for that is how their fathers treated the false prophets' (Lk 6:26).

If they speak well of you, then you may get the reputation of being the nicest Christian in the whole town who doesn't have an opinion about anything! People will speak well of you for a while, and you'll avoid attacks and persecution. But when the salt has lost its savour, it won't be good for anything except for being thrown out and trampled under the feet of man.

Spirit-filled Christians have avoided resistance and persecution. Some believers draw back and shake in their flesh, 'This way is too difficult. I am, after all, alone. I'll be isolated and won't have any friends. My children might even be affected.' Believe in Jesus and pray for protection instead. The devil can't touch you!

A man asked me this question once at the university: 'If I don't believe like you do, will I end up in hell?' 'Yes,' I answered. 'Next question, please!' He was speechless, because he never expected me to give that answer. At most, he probably expected me to sugarcoat the words. When he came to speak to me afterwards, I didn't feel any hate or aggression from him at all. Instead, I felt his respect. This happens when you are radical. You might also make some enemies, as Paul also stated, 'because a great door for effective work has opened to me, and there are many who oppose me' (1 Cor 16:9).

There will be those who don't like you, but you'll be respected in the spirit realm because you stand for Jesus Christ. When you run up against demons, they'll say: 'Jesus I know, and Johnson I also know, because he's always casting out demons where he lives in Pittsburgh!'

Paul was respected in the spirit realm. He was known of God, feared by demons and misunderstood by many people. It's better to be known by God and misunderstood by a few people, than to have favour with people and lose strength in the Spirit. What would you choose?

You might go through a period of isolation if you choose Jesus. Then you need to have the same attitude that Paul had. 'I asked no man, then I went my way.' He had an inner strength that enabled him to go it alone in the beginning, the middle and the end! I'm not talking about stubbornness and pride, but about standing on your own two feet in the Spirit and being independent in God. Do you understand the difference? When forced to choose between truth and fellowship, some always choose fellowship because they're afraid of being alone. When Paul was saved, all loneliness disappeared from his life for ever, because he was always busy following Jesus.

Resistance is part of the 'package'

When Paul and his team began to preach, they immediately experienced resistance and persecution. We believe in victory, open doors, enduring fruit, success, breakthroughs, and revival. Yet we aren't so naive as to think that we can get revival around a cup of tea, and that the world will applaud it. We know that things will become worse in the Last Days, but we don't need to suffer from a persecution complex. It is interesting to study Paul in this context:

> On the next Sabbath almost the whole city gathered to hear the word of the Lord. When the Jews saw the crowds, they were filled with jealousy and talked abusively against what Paul was saying . . . But the Jews incited the God-fearing women of high standing and the leading men of the city. They stirred up persecution against Paul and Barnabas, and expelled them from their region (Acts 13:44–45, 50).

This happened in Antioch, and it looks like a failure. Imagine if you were to travel to Kiev and have a campaign. Soon after setting up your tent or renting the stadium, you begin to preach. Suddenly, your opponents show up to drive you out of town! They chase you and throw stones at you. You go home and say that it was a total failure. However, Paul never says his campaign failed. He knew that he would encounter resistance wherever he went. He knew that it was part of the 'package' and that he had the power, strength and ability to overcome it.

I'm sure that many in Paul's position would immediately give up, go home and believe that they didn't have any anointing at all. There is a tendency to interpret resistance negatively as God's judgement over you or as proof that something is wrong. Instead, it is more often proof that something is right! You and I must strengthen ourselves spiritually to handle resistance. You cannot live in your Christian ivory tower, because tougher times will come. God can give you the spiritual strength that enables you to live in complicated situations without falling apart or running off to hide somewhere. Don't follow the example of one of Paul's co-workers, Demas, who left Paul for the cares of this world when things got too tough.

The gospel always has an impact!

At Iconium Paul and Barnabas went as usual into the Jewish synagogue. There they spoke so effectively that a great number of Jews and Gentiles believed. But the Jews who refused to believe stirred up the Gentiles and poisoned their minds against the brothers. So Paul and Barnabas spent considerable time there, speaking boldly for the Lord, who confirmed the message of his grace by enabling them to do miraculous signs and wonders. The people of the city were divided; some sided with the Jews, others with the apostles. There was a plot afoot among the Gentiles and Jews, together with their leaders, to mistreat them and stone them. But they found out about it and fled to the Lycaonian cities of Lystra and Derbe and to the surrounding country (Acts 14:1–6).

When Paul came to Iconium and started to preach, something suddenly happened in the spirit realm! The Jews who didn't want to listen stirred up the Gentiles and aroused their hatred towards the brothers. Chaos was everywhere, but Paul never let it bother him. He continued to preach for a while and God performed signs, wonders and acts of power. Suddenly the city began to boil. The people were divided into two camps, which made it impossible for Paul to preach. He then decided to move on to the next town.

This is what happened in the days of Paul. Jesus is our primary example, and Paul is our second. 'Do as I do,' he says.

When the preachers that John Wesley sent out returned, he asked them if they'd had any converts.

'No,' one preacher answered, 'I haven't had any saved.'

'Did you make anyone furious then?'

'Yes, some were terribly angry.'

'Then you've been doing a good job!'

You can praise God when people get furious with you, because things are really beginning to happen. This doesn't mean that you should go out and stir people up. The offence of the gospel cannot be reduced no matter how hard you try, if you're really preaching the gospel.

> Then some Jews came from Antioch and Iconium and won the crowd over. They stoned Paul and dragged him outside the city, thinking he was dead. But after the disciples had gathered around him, he got up and went back into the city. The next day he and Barnabas left for Derbe (Acts 14:19–20).

There are people in Uppsala who don't like Word of Life. They don't just stay in Uppsala, Sweden but travel to Stockholm and talk to the government and call journalists. They spread their aggression to as many as possible. This is what Paul had around him. When he came to Lystra and preached, what happened? A few fanatical Jews from Antioch and Iconium came after him and drew people over to their side. What a wonderful revival he must have had! Everyone was against him!

You shouldn't look for persecution or find any pleasure in it, but if you do anything for Jesus you will meet resistance. You need to learn to take it. If you say, 'God, make me like Paul,' expect some stone throwing! If you say, 'I feel that I have Paul's ministry for the Last Days,' then the stones will rain down on you. But you'll be raised from the dead like Paul, and you'll finish your race.

11

Independence – Paul's Driving Force and Attitude

> *But when God, who set me apart from birth and called me by his grace, was pleased to reveal his Son in me so that I might preach him among the Gentiles, I did not consult any man, nor did I go up to Jerusalem to see those who were apostles before I was, but I went immediately into Arabia and later returned to Damascus. Then after three years, I went up to Jerusalem to get acquainted with Peter and stayed with him fifteen days. I saw none of the other apostles only James, the Lord's brother* (Gal 1:15–19).

Paul continues:

> Fourteen years later I went up again to Jerusalem; this time with Barnabas. I took Titus along also. I went in response to a revelation and set before them the gospel that I preach among the Gentiles. But I did this privately to those who seemed to be leaders, for fear that I was running or had run my race in vain (Gal 2:1–2).

Independence given by the Holy Spirit is another aspect of the apostolic ministry. Jesus revealed himself to Paul when he was newly saved. 'I have not received this from any man,' he says. 'I have received it from God. Jesus revealed it to me.' Paul was independent because he was driven by the conviction of his calling, conversion and the revelation God placed in his heart.

This by no means implies that he was obstinate. We read how Paul reproaches the Corinthians for just this attitude:

> What I mean is this: One of you says, 'I follow Paul'; another, 'I follow Apollos'; another, 'I follow Cephas'; still another, 'I follow Christ' (1 Cor 1:12).

Paul is referring to people who aren't in fellowship with a church and who say: 'It's just God and me.' If you should ask them: 'Would you like to go out and witness?' they would answer: 'I have to ask Jesus first.' This improper, independent attitude causes isolation.

There are always 'other brothers'

A strong, independent ministry like Paul's always runs the risk of being misunderstood, falsely accused and isolated. Paul was first isolated in his home town of Tarsus. Barnabas had to find and take him to Jerusalem and Antioch. He later began the ministry to which he was called, yet he wasn't particularly thrilled about the idea of going to Jerusalem. Neither was he excited about having to prove to others how pure in doctrine he was, and what revelations he had. He was completely occupied with what Jesus had called him to do. This caused some problems because the others didn't really know what to do with this guy who wasn't from the 'Jerusalem gang'.

Remember that there are always 'other brothers'. When God tells you to do something, there are always others doing the same thing somewhere else in the world. When God gives you revelation you think is unique, there are always others who have received the same revelation. When people come and say, 'I have something that no one else has,' in all likelihood they haven't received anything at all!

Paul never said, 'Oh, those guys in Jerusalem are worthless. I am really the only one who's got it.' He wasn't that kind of person. He simply had the necessary independence in God that enabled him to accomplish the task, independent of others. Nevertheless, he realised that he needed to be in contact with the brothers in Jerusalem. They needed to understand him and relate to what he was doing.

You can be alone with Jesus

Lift up your eyes and see what God is preparing for the end times. You must be driven by something greater than all the wonderful meetings that affect and encourage you. You must be driven, even when you are alone. This is why you should be grateful for solitude. Don't just consult with people; have fellowship with Jesus! You'll never be alone again.

I haven't been alone since I was saved. Before I was saved, I felt alone and restless, although I had many friends. At times I felt shy and inhibited. I remember boarding a bus at home in Gothenburg. I felt as if everyone was watching me. I grabbed the first available seat and sat down as quickly as possible, so that no one would need to look at me.

Later, I got saved. I was just a babe in Christ when I was taken up to the platform to testify. When I stood behind the pulpit, something came over me. 'I feel good here!' I thought. Jesus broke the power of shyness that had kept me from looking people in the eye.

I experienced my first attack when I was just a few days old in the Lord. I was sitting in a bus when suddenly a thought struck me, 'There is no God.' Everything got dark. Up to this point the existence of God never came into question, because my conversion experience was so strong. The reassurance came, 'Of course he exists; I've been saved.' I then had a remarkable spiritual experience. It felt as if a hatch opened in my head and a light from heaven, coming from behind, radiated into my innermost being, into my soul. I was filled with the presence of God, and something left me and disappeared. I really don't know what it was, but I have never been alone from that moment. It was as if God set me free from a feeling of loneliness, anxiety and isolation.

This happened in May 1970. Since then, I haven't for a second felt what people call loneliness. It's wonderful to be alone, because then I can be with Jesus! I can enter a hotel room when I'm out preaching and say: 'Thank you Jesus for being here. No meeting and no preaching, just you and me.' Then the presence of God comes. I get on my knees, lie on the bed, sleep, wake up, continue to praise God and bask in his presence.

Fellowship in the Spirit

Paul had his own 'motor'. The revelation gave him an inner driving force that enabled him to enjoy being with the brothers, without becoming dependent upon them. There are many fine preachers who died, spiritually speaking, because of their dependence upon their brothers in Christ. I'm not talking about an independence that isolates you from others. It is wonderful to be with brothers in the Lord! When Paul finally arrived as a prisoner in Rome, or at the Three Taverns, he rejoiced and received new courage when he saw the brothers who had come to meet him (Acts 28:15).

How do you relate to others? Do you just greet their bodies, or are you only interested in their soulish intellect? Or do you communicate spirit to spirit? God, who is spirit, wants to have fellowship with you in your spirit. He also wants you to relate to others from your inner man. After all, the Bible does say that we should know each other by the spirit.

When I meet some people, there is something that lifts me and our spirits come in contact. 'You have refreshed my spirit,' Paul says. Unfortunately, some people don't refresh my spirit – they grieve my soul instead. Have you ever experienced this? It has nothing to do with depression, but with soulish or fleshly attitudes, selfishness, pride or conceit. These can be hidden behind a mask of religious terminology and shouts of 'Hallelujah' or 'Praise the Lord', but there is no contact in the spirit.

Don't compromise what has been revealed to you

There was a man in the Old Testament who became isolated and alone. His name was Joseph, and his brothers threw him into a well. Surely this was isolation! Why did it happen? Because God revealed to Joseph that they would one day bow before him, and they didn't like that. Joseph came to Potiphar, and was later thrown into prison. He was eventually restored and came into the promises of God.

Many years later, Joseph met his brothers again. There was now a time of famine and the land was desolate. The brothers came to Egypt to find food, and eventually found themselves standing before Joseph. Notice that Joseph didn't immediately open up and tell them who he was. He checked them out instead and listened. Did he do it judgementally or critically? No, not at all. When he saw that they had changed and regretted what they had done to him, then he knew the time was right to make contact. He opened his heart, cried, showed who he was and restored their relationship.

Joseph never compromised his position. He would have remained in solitude rather than have superficial fellowship with his brothers. When he saw the change in his brothers, he wanted to be with them again.

This is very important! There are many preachers who sell out on revelation, conviction and truth to get fellowship. Never do this! Maybe you're concerned about being rejected and persecuted, and being called a teacher of false doctrines. If so, you can say what Paul says: 'As the false teachers, but true!' It doesn't matter what people say. What does God say?

Some seek to bind your freedom

If you have something from God, then you have received it from God's Spirit, haven't you? And where the Spirit of the Lord is, there is liberty! I'm talking about spiritual liberty, not rebellion or freedom for your flesh. Spiritual freedom is like standing on a limitless horizon, in a wide-open place, as David writes in Psalm 18:19. This is the freedom to prophesy, preach, lay hands on the sick, and to let the Holy Spirit come upon you. This freedom is wonderful.

God wants you to have freedom in every area, even though there are those who hate this freedom. We can read in Galatians about the 'brothers' who slipped into the church to bind their freedom

(Gal 2:4). They did this because they hadn't paid the price to discard worldliness, the fear of man and their secret ambitions. God doesn't want you to have secret ambitions. He wants you to live in the light. You shouldn't live according to a double standard and walk on two paths, even if only one is visible. You will have more freedom if you keep to one path alone.

Those who bind your freedom don't like this. When someone is healed, or when the Holy Spirit comes upon you, or when you cast out an evil spirit, they get angry and want to cast you out of the church! There is, in almost every moderately alive church, at least one senior citizen whom no one really understands. People have always thought that he was a little strange. 'This is Jones, he's a little odd. He prophesies and does unusual things. We put up with him because he's a relic from the old days.' It's true that he's a relic from the old days, and he's the only one who has any life left in him! The others have conformed, compromised and become faded and grey. Praise God for senior citizens who prophesy! But they are always bound and despised by carnal individuals who don't understand how the Holy Spirit flows and functions. No one has the right to sit in judgement over spiritual manifestations!

There are always those who want to 'be careful' and take it easy. 'What are the others saying? They're limiting my freedom so I'd better take it easy for a while.' No! Even if they limit your freedom, don't let them take it from you completely! Paul was great because he never backed down.

> We did not give in to them for a moment, so that the truth of the gospel might remain with you. As for those who seemed to be important – whatever they were makes no difference to me; God does not judge by external appearance – those men added nothing to my message (Gal 2:5–6).

Never betray the truth for the sake of fellowship

There was no fear or false respect in Paul, but neither did he preach rebellion. I've noticed at times a kind of nonchalant rebellion among believers and even preachers. They put down other ministers, always speak badly of some or put pressure on them. You never find these tendencies in Paul. He even demonstrated respect for an unrighteous high priest when he realised that he was being confronted by him (Acts 23:1–5). You should do the same. You should accept, love and respect ministers and all authority placed over you.

> When Peter came to Antioch, I opposed him to his face, because he was clearly in the wrong. Before certain men came from James, he used to eat with the Gentiles. But when they arrived, he began to draw back and separate himself from the Gentiles because he was afraid of those who belonged to the circumcision group.... When I saw that they were not acting in line with the truth of the gospel, I said to Peter in front of them all, 'You are a Jew, yet you live like a Gentile and not like a Jew. How is it, then, that you force Gentiles to follow Jewish customs?' (Gal 2:11–12,14).

Paul was bold and independent in God. Truth was important to him, not fellowship. Some preachers are always looking for some little group that they can hook up with, a group they can enter into and feel accepted. 'I could really be something here!' This attitude has got to stop. Know what God has given you and thank him for it. Do what you are supposed to do, reap the harvest, and grow and walk worthy of the gospel of truth. Be part of what God is doing, but never compromise the truth for fellowship.

Didn't Peter lose respect for Paul when he was openly confronted? No, not at all. In Peter's last letter, he writes about his beloved brother Paul and his letters:

> ...just as our dear brother Paul also wrote to you with the wisdom that God gave him. He writes the same way in all his letters, speaking in them of these matters. His letters contain some things that are hard to understand...(2 Pet 3:15–16).

Peter simply says that Paul is difficult to understand at times. There may be ministries you can't understand, but they still come from God.

Some preach because of envy and strife

We may not always understand what God has called someone else to do, nor does God give us this responsibility. When you receive something from heaven, be sure to carry it out with the conviction that you are obeying Jesus' command. Otherwise you may feel like a martyr when others don't understand what you're doing. Some may not understand now, but they will. Others may take a while longer to understand, and a few never will. There is a special perseverance and patience that enables you to bless and stay at peace with everyone. Then you can still do what you're supposed to without having to defend yourself. We defend the gospel, not ourselves or our ministries.

Paul had this boldness and strength throughout his life. He was sitting in prison when he wrote the letter to the Philippians. He preached in many churches and even started some of them, and yet he finished in jail. Paul spent more time in prison than he did the Hilton, but that never slowed down the progress of the gospel.

> Now I want you to know, brothers, that what has happened to me has really served to advance the gospel. As a result, it has become clear throughout the whole palace guard and to everyone else that I am in chains for Christ. Because of my chains, most of the brothers in the Lord have been encouraged to speak the word of God more courageously and fearlessly (Phil 1:12–14).

Paul was an example in all things. He didn't get depressed when he was thrown into prison. He took the opportunity to preach, defend, establish and pray for the gospel. He was extremely bold!

In verse 15 of the same chapter, Paul says that 'some indeed preach Christ even from envy and strife'. Paul was called and sent out to preach Christ, but he wasn't alone. Others did the same. At times, Paul preached with some of them while others preached independently of him. Some followed him with the intention of destroying what he had built up. After Paul visited the church in Galatia, it didn't take long until Judaisers came and created confusion. 'Who is this Paul? You must be circumcised; you must keep the law!'

The greatest attacks against Paul's ministry came from the so-called Judaisers, and secondly from the Jews who didn't believe that Jesus was the Messiah. There were Judaised Jewish believers who didn't understand Paul, so they travelled around twisting everything he said. You may be asked to speak a truth, and then someone will come up beside you and say: 'Yes, I agree with you, but...' And so they twist everything you say until it's completely different from what God said to you. They twist and distort what you say because they're jealous.

Conflicts arise in every revival

Paul is in prison. 'Wonderful,' they think. 'Surely God has condemned him for all the damage he's caused! Thank God he's finally caught! Now we can sort everything out.' What does Paul say?

> It is true that some preach Christ out of envy and rivalry, but others out of goodwill. The latter do so in love, knowing that I am put here for the defence of the gospel. The former preach Christ out of selfish ambition, not sincerely, supposing that they can stir up trouble for me while I am in chains (Phil 1:15–17).

Disturbances always appear as soon as there is revival. Preachers start to stab each other in the back, and the people say: 'If the preachers can't get along, then how can they expect us to?' There will always be a degree of turmoil and conflict in every revival. Sin and the flesh rise up, but God is greater!

Paul says:

> In the first place, I hear that when you come together as a church, there are divisions among you, and to some extent I believe it. No doubt there have to be differences among you to show which of you have God's approval (1 Cor 11:18–19).

We aren't perfect when God calls us, but he does give us a measure of grace and anointing and begins to work with us. Our consciences aren't always clean in every area; there are underlying motives and thoughts that do not come from God. Different situations cause them to surface, which is good because they can be dealt with instead of being repressed. It then becomes apparent who makes the grade. It's easy to see what's on the inside when things get tough.

Paul continues:

> But what does it matter? The important thing is that in every way, whether from false motives or true, Christ is preached. And because of this I rejoice. Yes, and I will continue to rejoice, for I know that through your prayers and the help given by the Spirit of Jesus Christ, what has happened to me will turn out for my deliverance (Phil 1:18–19).

Paul also says: 'I do what I'm called to do. I remain in him and make sure to spend time with Jesus. I want you to pray that the Spirit of God will come upon me, and that I'll have a proper and relaxed attitude as I complete my work for the Lord.'

You need faith to overcome attacks

Earlier, we read that Paul was alone at the beginning of his ministry. He was often alone in prison during the middle of his ministry years. When he was outside prison, many strange things happened that he had no control over. Things will also happen that you have no control over. Pray, but not like this: 'God, make them do what I want. Let my will be done, in Jesus' name!' This is witchcraft! Cast your cares on the Lord instead.

You need faith, not just for healing or financial provision. You need faith from heaven to deal with difficult situations and attacks against the church. You need faith to hear from the Holy Spirit, so that you won't just listen to people and do what they do. You can make bad choices if you're just looking for a little appreciation from people. You need faith for every situation.

> For I am already being poured out like a drink offering, and the time has come for my departure. I have fought the good fight, I have finished the race, I have kept the faith. Now there is in store for me the crown of righteousness, which the Lord, the righteous Judge, will award to me on that day – and not only to me, but also to all who have longed for his appearing (2 Tim 4:6 8).

'I am finished,' Paul said. 'I've now completed what Jesus asked me to do when he appeared to me on the road to Damascus. I've completed what Jesus told me to do as I fell into a trance in the temple in Jerusalem. I finished what Jesus said I would do as a prisoner in Jerusalem, and on the way to Caesarea and Rome. Everything he told me to do has now been completed. The work is over, everything is done. Now I can leave for heaven!' Doesn't this sound wonderful! Every Christian should be able to say the same.

Paul – independent to the end

Afterwards, Paul writes something remarkable to Timothy:

> Do your best to come to me quickly, for Demas, because he loved this world, has deserted me and has gone to Thessalonica. . . . Only Luke is with me (2 Tim 4:9–11).

Eventually, people started to leave Paul. He speaks later of those who hurt him, like Alexander the coppersmith (v 14). He also says that the entire province of Asia has left him, even the churches he founded. They were no longer with him, but against him. Did this affect the way he thought? Do we see a bitter, old Paul? Not at all!

> At my first defence, no one came to my support, but everyone deserted me. May it not be held against them. But the Lord stood at my side and gave me strength, so that through me the message might be fully proclaimed and all the Gentiles might hear it. And I was delivered from the lion's mouth. The Lord will rescue me from every evil attack and will bring me safely to his heavenly kingdom. To him be glory for ever and ever. Amen (2 Tim 4:16–18).

The Christians who should have been Paul's help and strength in his last hours, abandoned him. But he says: 'I have finished my race. I have preached and everyone has left me. But do you know what, Timothy? I had the chance to preach the gospel. I had the opportunity to preach everywhere among the Gentiles, even in court!'

We cannot find a trace of personal ambition, bitterness, disappointment, depression or a desire for power. Just a free apostle, called and used by God, who has fulfilled his office.

'But didn't you fail, Paul? Your churches are in a mess. What will happen to them? Some of your disciples have left you and become worldly. Imagine the crowds you could have preached to in Rome. They won't even listen to you now. Haven't you failed?'

'Failed? I have completed my race! I've won the victory, and my crown of victory awaits!'

This is an apostle! This is a man driven by an inner force, who has heard from heaven. He has followed the vision and revelation and been led by the Holy Spirit. This is a man with a strong, genuine independence, who didn't work for man, but God. He didn't receive the praise of men, but said: 'You cannot judge me; I don't even judge myself. God is my judge and he will reward me for what I have done. I know that I have finished my race!'

God wants ministers like this throughout the world!

12

Paul – Our Example

Are you beginning to like Paul? He's fantastic! When you understand his heart, you will understand what he is saying. You'll understand statements such as:

> But even if we or an angel from heaven should preach a gospel other than the one we preached to you, let him be eternally condemned! (Gal 1:8).

When you understand Paul's heart, you'll realise why he had to warn, correct and punish. You need to understand how he functioned.

It's wonderful to read about Paul, his calling and his life. He was like a lion of God, and a punch-bag for the devil! The devil hit him all the time, but he always came back. Paul is perfectly described in Proverbs 24:16: 'For though a righteous man falls seven times, he rises again, but the wicked are brought down by calamity'. When some fall, they remain on the ground for the rest of their lives. Not Paul. When he was almost stoned to death, he got up, shook off the stones and went back into town to preach!

Paul not only led and cleared the way for others, but he was an example for us all. In Acts we read:

> So be on your guard! Remember that for three years I never stopped warning each of you night and day with tears' . . . I have not coveted anyone's silver or gold or clothing. You yourselves know that these hands

of mine have supplied my own needs and the needs of my companions. In everything I did, I showed you that by this kind of hard work we must help the weak, remembering the words the Lord Jesus himself said: 'It is more blessed to give than to receive' (Acts 20:31, 33–35).

Every apostle and believer should provide such an example. Remember, you are always an example to someone.

No one is perfect

When we talk about being examples, you might think: 'I have so many weaknesses. I can't be an example for anyone!' Yes, you can. If you're honest and have a pure heart, then God will do something wonderful with you. He will hide your weaknesses!

God is never interested in exposing your weaknesses to everyone. The Holy Spirit is a gentleman. Jesus loves you, and has confidence in you and works with you in secret. However, if you are nonchalant, have wrong motives and an impure heart, then your weaknesses will be exposed. No one is perfect, not even Paul. We can see this when Paul worked with Barnabas. Barnabas wanted to take John Mark along on their next trip (Acts 15:36–41).

'John Mark?' thundered Paul. 'Not on your life! He's out of the question!'

'Oh no,' countered Barnabas. 'John Mark is a fine person.'

'Fine? Last time he took off and left us. He stayed with us as far as Cyprus, then headed for home again. I won't take John Mark. I want someone I can trust, like Silas. He's better.'

'But I feel that we should take John Mark with us,' said Barnabas.

'All right, then you can take him!'

The Bible says that there was a dispute between them. A dispute occurs when one blames another. Barnabas and Paul argued. Paul was stubborn, and he didn't like John Mark. He took Silas instead, and he and Barnabas parted company. God used the situation anyway. I think the incident caused God to smile a little. He divided Paul and Barnabas, and they took their own territories. So, in spite of their weaknesses, God used them.

When Paul was older, he wrote in his second letter to Timothy: 'Come to me, because only Luke is still with me, and bring with you John Mark. He will be useful to have here!' (2 Tim 4:11).

What happened? John Mark shaped up! Perhaps you're a pastor of a church with many co-workers. Some are on the ball, some aren't. Some are awake while others sleep. Do you know what? They can shape up as well! Something happened to John Mark that caused him to change. It took a few years, but he developed and matured. He got his act together; so much so that he was later used by God to write one of the gospels. Not bad! Maybe Paul didn't understand him and became impatient. Paul changed as well. He might have been too rigid at first. As Paul matured and grew older, he became more charitable.

Remember that people change. Don't hold their old mistakes against them, because we all make mistakes and say foolish things. Sort it out with God, and don't hold it against them. Keeping resentment in your heart towards someone is the surest way to wreck your ministry. The Lord reminded me of a person that I became irritated with a few years ago. 'What did you argue about?' the Holy Spirit asked. I couldn't even remember!

Preach and be an example

You have difficulties and Paul had difficulties. We aren't talking about perfect people, but committed individuals with pure hearts. Paul is a perfect example of this.

All instruction comes two ways: partly through teaching, and partly by example. God has always done it this way. The absence of role models is the greatest deficiency in society today.

The absence of good role models creates poor role models. Look at the idols of the music industry. They exist because people are looking for examples to follow. It isn't wrong to have a role model, but it is wrong to have an idol. Never put a person on a pedestal.

There is even a lack of role models in the body of Christ. Without them, we won't have examples to follow. It is vital to realise that following Christ is associated with following Jesus' servants. Paul says in 1 Corinthians 4:16–17:

> I urge you to imitate me. For this reason I am sending to you Timothy, my son whom I love, who is faithful in the Lord. He will remind you of my way of life in Christ Jesus, which agrees with what I teach everywhere in every church.

Paul is relating the gospel and its proclamation with the one proclaiming it. They cannot be divided.

I remember a preacher who came to me during the time I was reading Kenneth Hagin's books. He said: 'You can preach about faith, but don't mention Hagin's name. This way you'll avoid a lot of persecution and people will receive what you teach. You don't have to name him. He's just a man.' No! If we receive a God-given message, but are ashamed of the servant God chooses to deliver it, then we are ashamed of God. They cannot be separated. Paul is our greatest example in this area.

You can have a clear conscience

> Surely you remember, brothers, our toil and hardship; we worked night and day in order not to be a burden to anyone while we preached the gospel of God to you. You are witnesses, and so is God, of how holy, righteous and blameless we were among you who believed (1 Thess 2:9–10).

> Paul looked straight at the Sanhedrin and said, 'My brothers, I have fulfilled my duty to God in all good conscience to this day' (Acts 23:1).

Paul had a clear understanding of righteousness from God. 'I have walked before God every day with a clear conscience,' he says. Does that mean he never made any mistakes? No, but he was convinced that the blood of Jesus cleansed him from sin. When the blood of Jesus cleanses you, your sins are obliterated. You no longer have a burden of sin, so you never need to wonder if you're doing what is right or wrong.

I learned something interesting during my military service. They said: 'It's better to give a bad order than no order at all!' If you are a Christian leader constantly plagued by uncertainty, then

Jesus wants to set you free. Many spiritual leaders in my country are bound because they are tormented in their conscience, and unsure of God's love for them. You need to be bold and secure in God. Remember that God loves you and will use you, though you are far from perfect. But, in Jesus you are perfect! This means that like Paul, you can claim to have a clear conscience every day.

You can have a clear conscience! When you do, you'll be happy and relaxed. You can get through many difficulties and solve many problems, without losing courage and becoming paralysed. You can always hear from heaven, and know what to do. If you have a clear conscience, then you'll be as bold as Paul. I know of no other, except the Lord himself, who was so bold. 'Be as I am,' Paul said. 'I have walked among you with a good conscience and have done a holy work. I have not hidden what I have done, nor done it in secret. Instead of taking your money, I have worked more than the others. I am holy and clean before God, and I want you to follow my example!'

God wants a generation of role models

Your parents were your role models when you were a child. You saw what Mum and Dad did. Many say that they had bad parents, but they don't know what they are saying. You should bless your parents with all of your heart, no matter how imperfect they were! Somehow, they were still role models and examples.

God uses role models to teach us, but the devil has taken this away from the body of Christ. Many of those who come into the church have their eyes on the world and the world's methods. The world is their role model. How wrong! This is why God needs to raise up role models in the Holy Spirit. They aren't perfect, but they work!

If you study the body of Christ in the light of history, you'll see that very much didn't work. One reason is that preachers didn't stand up and become role models because of false modesty and shyness. God wants a generation of role models, not just followers. He wants you to be a role model, whether you're an apostle or not. But the apostolic ministry must be an example.

> What you heard from me, keep as the pattern of sound teaching, with faith and love in Christ Jesus (2 Tim 1:13).

> And the things you have heard me say in the presence of many witnesses entrust to reliable men who will also be qualified to teach others (2 Tim 2:2).

Many books are being written today, but don't just look at the content. It's also interesting to study the lives of the authors. They should live as they teach. If a preacher talks about faith, then he should live by faith. He shouldn't only live in faith during his twenty-minute sermon, and then retreat into a life of fear and confusion. The absence of role models in the body of Christ is causing confusion about what believers should do and who they should follow. Believers have become easily impressed with everything that comes their way, and naively think that everything is great. Then we wonder why they run after something that isn't from God. They never learned how to live from role models.

When I attended Bible school, the Holy Spirit spoke to me and said: 'Don't learn through the teaching you hear alone, but learn also by example. Watch how ministries flow and operate.' I've travelled with many preachers since then. After one preacher said something I didn't agree with, the Holy Spirit said: 'Don't worry about what he said. Observe the spirit behind him. See how he functions, watch what he does.' I learned by example! When people won't learn by example in the local church, the devil comes instead and causes grief and misery.

There are those who want a train of followers trailing after them. There are travelling preachers who always want a group with them for prayer support or to lead the worship. Actually, they may have the impure motive of needing to be surrounded by a group of admirers. Travel alone first, and learn to do the work correctly, then you can take your group of co-workers! You don't need cheerleaders around you to cheer you on and puff up your ego.

Learn from your leaders

You, however, know all about my teaching, my way of life, my purpose, faith, patience, love, endurance, persecutions, sufferings –

what kinds of things happened to me in Antioch, Iconium and Lystra, the persecutions I endured. Yet the Lord rescued me from all of them. In fact, everyone who wants to live a godly life in Christ Jesus will be persecuted, while evil men and imposters will go from bad to worse, deceiving and being deceived. But as for you, continue in what you have learned and have become convinced of, because you know those from whom you learned it (2 Tim 3:10-14).

What is a role model? It isn't necessarily someone you generally like, or find interesting or fun to be with, but someone God has chosen. God chose Paul for Timothy. The Holy Spirit told him to 'Watch, follow, see why he does this or that.' Life itself provides most of your teaching. This is why you must first accept the fact that God has placed the pastor and leaders in the church you attend. Secondly, you must respect the positions they have and, thirdly, regard them as role models. This doesn't mean that you copy everything they do, but follow them as they follow Jesus. You'll soon begin to wonder what motivates them, why they make certain decisions and so on. The Holy Spirit will then teach you things you could never learn from the pulpit.

The ministry gifts don't just pop up automatically: 'Everything's ready. I haven't had fellowship with anyone because I've got everything directly from God without any role models!' They grow and mature in relationships with others, or under someone else's ministry.

Paul spent time serving and receiving things from Barnabas. Paul eventually came into his own ministry, but first he had role models. We should also.

Your life should pass inspection

We are no longer following Christ if we move away from good role models, because we automatically find poor ones. Music has provided examples of this, even if times are changing. Some Christian musicians and singers have sung songs about God, while their lives haven't reflected the words. Yet, they may be extremely popular. Why? Because they are not 'salt' and they are not challenging their audience. Large crowds are drawn to their concerts, but what happens? The concerts are filled with confusion and all kinds of evil!

Musicians are often the role models for young people. That's why we see youngsters going around with rings in their ears and torn jeans. Our role models should be ministers. You might say: 'Of course, but some musicians are ministers!' Well then, make sure that they really are ministers, and that they live like ministers! The body of Christ needs role models. It needs people who have heard from God and live with God, who dare to say: 'Do as I do and think as I think!'

> Finally, brothers, whatever is true, whatever is noble, whatever is right, whatever is pure, whatever is lovely, whatever is admirable – if anything is excellent or praiseworthy – think about such things. Whatever you have learned or received or heard from me, or seen in me – put it into practice. And the God of peace will be with you (Phil 4:8–9).

It may be hard for you to imagine Paul saying that they should do everything he has preached and done, so that the peace of God will be with them. When were you last at a meeting where the preacher stood up and said: 'Do as I do and everything will be all right!'? We seldom hear things like this, but we will in the future. People will grow in holiness, boldness and maturity and dare to be examples. They will dare to let others inspect their lives, because their lives will pass inspection in every area.

God wants you to be the same. He wants you to be an example in the Holy Spirit, so that people will say: 'I don't really like him, but one thing is certain: he believes in what he is doing and you can't find fault in him.'

13

The Proof of an Apostle – Signs and Wonders

Paul was saved through a supernatural revelation. While he was on the way to Damascus to persecute and imprison believers, the Lord revealed himself to Paul. We read that he fell from his horse and became blind from the radiance around him. He then heard a voice:

> 'Saul, Saul, why do you persecute me?' 'Who are you Lord?' Saul asked. 'I am Jesus, whom you are persecuting,' he replied (Acts 9:4–5).

We can read about the way Paul was saved and called in Acts 9, 22 and 26. These three chapters tell a completely supernatural story from beginning to end! This is because the church is supernatural.

The birth of the church is described in Acts 1 and 2. Fifty days after Passover, the Holy Spirit filled the room where the apostles were gathered. A loud noise came from heaven and tongues of fire sat on each of them, and they began to speak in new tongues. Accused of drunken behaviour, yet full of the Holy Spirit, they went out into the streets and filled Jerusalem with the sound of tongues. The church had been born through the Holy Spirit's baptism and outpouring over the believers. Tongues were now heard throughout Jerusalem!

The Holy Spirit and the supernatural are the characteristics and strength of the church, not our intellect, ability, willpower, emotions or experience!

> I must go on boasting. Although there is nothing to be gained, I will go on to visions and revelations from the Lord (2 Cor 12:1).

Visions and revelations came to Paul regularly during his life and ministry. They came when he needed instructions for his calling. Jesus was constantly revealing himself to Paul.

There are two pitfalls to avoid concerning visions and revelations. The first is when people fear these experiences and believe that something must be wrong if someone has a vision. The other occurs when people seek revelations to the degree that they leave everything else and become over-spiritual! The church is informed and led by visions and revelations, so God wants you to avoid both errors. His Holy Spirit speaks through the supernatural, so it is an inextricable part of the church and vital for its life.

Miracles followed Paul everywhere

> I have made a fool of myself, but you drove me to it. I ought to have been commended by you, for I am not in the least inferior to the 'super apostles', even though I am nothing (2 Cor 12:11).

Paul feels the need to speak as a fool. Others had come to draw the Corinthians away from the teaching he gave them. Therefore, he is forced to explain who he is and what God has given him, so the Corinthians won't lose confidence in him.

In Acts 20:29, Paul says that 'savage wolves' will come in among the believers in Ephesus and not spare the flock after he leaves. Paul learned this the hard way. So will you, if you choose to work for God! The devil will always try to be ahead of you to prevent you from reaching your destination. Once you've arrived, he tries to destroy what you are doing. He will then twist and confuse everything you've done after you've left. Paul's strength was the Holy Spirit.

> The things that mark an apostle – signs, wonders and miracles – were done among you with great perseverance (2 Cor 12:12).

Signs and wonders are part of the proof of an apostolic ministry. Paul preached the gospel wherever he went. People were saved almost everywhere and the devil always opposed him! People were either for or against Paul, but God strengthened him. While he was in Corinth, Jesus came to him in a vision and said:

> 'Do not be afraid; keep on speaking, do not be silent. For I am with you, and no one is going to attack and harm you, because I have many people in this city' (Acts 18:9–10).

'I will strengthen you, I'll be with you, I'll help you in every way and encourage you.' Jesus continually says this to Paul, strengthening and encouraging him by revelation so that he can continue. And everywhere Paul travelled, signs confirmed his ministry. The kingdom of God manifested with signs, wonders and healing wherever he went.

The authorities need the word of God

In Acts 13, Saul and Barnabas are on their way to Cyprus after being sent from Antioch. John Mark was with them. It says in verse 5 that when they had come to Salamis, they preached the word of God in the Jewish synagogues:

> They travelled through the whole island until they came to Paphos. There they met a Jewish sorcerer and false prophet named Bar-Jesus, who was an attendant of the proconsul, Sergius Paulus. The proconsul, an intelligent man, sent for Barnabas and Saul because he wanted to hear the word of God (Acts 13:6–7).

People are always hungry for the word of God. This is particularly true of people in positions of authority, because they realise how incredibly difficult it is to fulfil their responsibilities in their own strength. They usually have a tremendous hunger for more power and blessing. They don't know where to get it, so they often turn to the nearest source. The devil always seeks high positions, partly because he once fell from a throne. Since then, he has worked to establish other thrones and continually tries to move up.

Magicians still exist today. They are people with occult abilities derived from their association with demons. Unfortunately, they are often found close to those with political power or influence.

Their aim is to increase the devil's influence over the earth. This is why Paul frequently had contact with the authorities, often at trials. God wants the authorities to hear his word, so they will go in the right direction.

Some Christians have read what Paul says in 1 Corinthians 1:26–29, and concluded that people who are in high positions rarely get saved. This is why Christians have focused on others in society. But the gospel must reach everyone! It's wonderful when Mr Smith gets saved, but it's also wonderful when someone in the government gets saved. 'All are equal in God's sight,' you say. Yes, they are, but many more are affected when a person in authority gets saved. Never disregard any class or group of people. God has called us to preach the gospel to members of the government as well as alcoholics and drug addicts.

God wants to perform miracles everywhere

When Paul approached Proconsul Sergius Paulus, Bar-Jesus the wizard – or Elymas as he was also called – was nearby. Paul's first miracle was somewhat different from what might have been expected. Filled with the Holy Spirit, Paul fixed his eyes on the wizard and said: 'You child of the devil!' What an introduction! People usually have preconceived ideas about what it means to be filled with the Holy Spirit, and the consequent signs, wonders and acts of power. Yet the supernatural can be shown in many ways.

When the Holy Spirit came upon Paul, he exposed an evil influence on authority.

'You are a child of the devil and an enemy of everything that is right! You are full of all kinds of deceits and trickery. Will you never stop perverting the right ways of the Lord? Now the hand of the Lord is against you. You are going to be blind, and for a time you will be unable to see the light of the sun.' Immediately mist and darkness came over him, and he groped about, seeking someone to lead him by the hand (Acts 13:10–11).

Imagine Paul's satisfaction in saying this! He knew what happened when he was saved. Elymas wasn't struck with sickness, nor was

Paul when he was blinded. He was blinded by a powerful light. It took just a little of God's glory to totally shake him!

You can withstand a great deal of God's glory if you have a right relationship with God. If you don't, then it's like sticking your fingers into an electric outlet. You'll feel it! But if you insert a plug into the outlet instead, then you can use the electricity for anything you want.

In other words, if you have the wrong 'relationship' to the electricity in the wires, you'll feel the results. God's glory is the same. When Paul, then called Saul, had a wrong relationship to God, he experienced the glory in a certain way. Now, Elymas the wizard had a similar experience:

> Immediately mist and darkness came over him, and he groped about, seeking someone to lead him by the hand. When the proconsul saw what had happened, he believed, for he was amazed at the teaching about the Lord (Acts 13:11–12).

He wasn't convinced intellectually, but by a sign. If God did this for the authorities then, he can do the same today. Wonders will take place. There are officials today like Sergius Paulus and their co-workers have the heart of the wizard, Elymas. But the Holy Spirit will separate them. And he will do this through signs and wonders. God wants you to have faith for miracles in your town, in your church and in the corridors of power, so that people will be shaken and saved!

Expect signs and wonders!

When the gospel enters a place for the first time, you should seek God and expect signs, wonders and acts of power. Jesus said that those who believe in him will cast out evil spirits, speak in new tongues, and lay hands on the sick (Mk 16:15–18). He didn't limit this command to the twelve or the seventy, but gave it to all believers:

> I tell you the truth, anyone who has faith in me will do what I have been doing. He will do even greater things than these, because I am going to the Father (Jn 14:12).

Jesus says that this promise applies to everyone. Of course, this includes the ministry gifts, but 'everyone' also means you. You should expect God to keep his promise. If you come into a situation where the gospel has hardly been preached, ask God for the keys to the people's hearts. These keys are signs, wonders and acts of power.

People expect the supernatural, which comes either from the devil and the occult, or from Jesus Christ. Signs and wonders belong to every believer, and not only the evangelist. They belong to every ministry gift, and definitely to the apostle. God wants to break through so that no one can doubt that his power is greater and more glorious than all human or occult power. The war that is raging in the spirit realm will become more real to us. Battles similar to those between Elijah and the prophets of Baal, and between Moses and the Egyptian wizards will again take place.

In Europe and the former Soviet Union, there are already contests between true and false signs and wonders. How tragic when the church is bound by fear, refusing anything to do with the miraculous or supernatural! As the church retreats in this area, the devil takes over. God doesn't want this, so expect signs and wonders!

Believers sometimes say things like, 'That's fine on the mission field, in Africa or Eastern Europe, but it is so hard here at home.' Why is it so hard? Because people are full of unbelief, wrong teaching or pride, and they are unwilling to receive. However, no walls are too hard for the Holy Spirit to break through.

Sometimes, we think it's difficult to see signs or wonders because people are so negative. Think about Jesus! He was often surrounded by a crowd of Pharisees, and all of them were mad at him. The Bible says that even Jesus got angry (Mk 3:5) and said to the man with the withered hand, 'Stretch out your hand.' The man was healed in front of the Pharisees, in an atmosphere of total unbelief. The signs and wonders Paul saw sometimes occurred while stones were being thrown at him!

The supernatural – a 'key' for your city

Many wonders that took place in Paul's ministry were 'keys' and they had two purposes. One was to demonstrate the love of Jesus to the sick by healing them. The other was to show that a miracle could be something more, a key. The woman at the well was the key to an entire city. The Holy Spirit gave Jesus a word of knowledge and exposed her whole life. This opened the entire city to the gospel! I am convinced that God wants to do the same today. There are still 'key wonders' for Uppsala that we haven't seen or experienced yet. The same is true for your town, so don't give up. This is especially true for pastors. Ask God for the key to an area and he will eventually show it to you. When this happens, the devil will usually become angry. He wants us to forget about wonders and not even mention them by name. The wonders that took place in the book of Acts were written down so that we would never forget them.

A few years ago, Word of Life was attacked and accused by the communists, the organisations for the disabled, the hospital and the School Board in Uppsala. Do you know what God did? He poured his Holy Spirit over a former communist, who was a handicapped person, working at the hospital and also on the School Board! God's combination was perfect. This person was changed so completely that the people in the various areas were shocked. Remember, God does whatever he wants!

Examine your motives

Expect signs and wonders when you move out as a pioneer! However, never try to force a miracle out of a person: 'Now I'm going to pray for you and I expect to see a miracle!' The right motives are really important. Why do we act as we do? Because Jesus loves people, and he wants to show them his glory, his power and his presence. He wants people to receive the full gospel.

This is why we can't preach the gospel without signs and wonders. Jesus loves the entire person – spirit, soul and body. The new birth takes place in the spirit. Restoration and healing apply to the soul, just as physical healing relates to the body. There is also healing for every situation in life. Remember that signs and wonders exist to glorify Jesus and to help people.

Preachers can sometimes be tempted to wallow in the glory that comes from heaven. Think about the day Jesus rode into Jerusalem on the donkey. He sat on the donkey's colt and people threw down their mantles and waved palm branches. The animal was ecstatic: 'I've never received so much attention in my life! I didn't know that I was so famous!' The donkey forgot that it was all for the Person on its back. You should always examine your motives when you invite people to receive salvation and when you pray for them. Their salvation should be your motivation. This is why we're happy when only one is saved, although it's wonderful when 500 are saved.

If your heart is right, you'll never be disappointed. You won't be frustrated, but grateful for what Jesus is doing. You won't end up under the curse of comparison, and you'll have the right motives for whatever you do. The purpose is to help people. 'This is God's love and power for this person. These signs and wonders touch these people, and I minister to them because Jesus loves them.' Then God will continually perform new signs and wonders.

Help people expect miracles

> In Lystra there sat a man crippled in his feet, who was lame from birth and had never walked. He listened to Paul as he was speaking. Paul looked directly at him, saw that he had faith to be healed and called out, 'Stand up on your feet!' At that, the man jumped up and began to walk (Acts 14:8–10).

When Paul and Barnabas preached the gospel, they preached it in such a way that the impotent man received faith to be healed. You cannot preach the gospel without telling people that they can be healed. Paul was convinced that Jesus healed. Peter was sure that Jesus healed. Jesus heals, and we need to tell people so.

If you preach the gospel as Paul did, people will hear that they can be healed and they will receive the faith for it. One of the reasons for the lack of signs and wonders is the tradition of unbelief that has existed in the pulpit. Yet the people haven't disbelieved! As a preacher, you don't have the right to raise objections to healing, because the Bible says that Jesus healed everyone who came to him. Ask God for forgiveness if you have had reservations about healing!

'But I've prayed for people who weren't visibly healed.' Does this change the word of God? No, but it may show that you've misunderstood the word of God. When you obey God's word and encounter resistance, God can show you the reason for the resistance. But you shouldn't run from difficulties by hiding behind disobedience and disbelief.

When Paul preached, he spoke in such a way that people expected to be healed. When Peter preached the first time to the Gentiles, he said:

> You know what has happened throughout Judea, beginning in Galilee after the baptism that John preached – how God anointed Jesus of Nazareth with the Holy Spirit and power, and how he went around doing good and healing all who were under the power of the devil, because God was with him (Acts 10:37–38).

The first thing that Peter preached to the Gentiles was that Jesus wanted to heal everyone. You must do the same and give them the full gospel.

Have the right motives and be filled with God's love for people. Know that miracles are the keys into circumstances that can change the entire spiritual atmosphere. God will then perform signs, wonders and acts of power through you!

14

The Apostle's Goal – Lasting Fruit

*And Jesus came and spoke to them, saying, 'All authority has been
given to Me in heaven and on earth. Go therefore and make disciples
of all the nations, baptizing them in the name of the Father and of the
Son and of the Holy Spirit, teaching them to observe all things that I
have commanded you; and lo, I am with you always, even to the end of
the age.' Amen (Mt 28:18–20 NKJV).*

All authority in heaven and on earth is given to Jesus. This means
that he can change anything and move anything. He proved this
through his resurrection and by walking through closed doors. He
does what he wants! He says:

I am He who lives, and was dead, and behold, I am alive forevermore.
Amen. And I have the keys of Hades and of Death (Rev 1:18 NKJV).

Nothing can hinder or stop Jesus from Nazareth. There are no
closed doors. They may seem closed before your eyes, but there is
nothing that Jesus can't walk through in the Spirit.

An apostle's work is never finished

I have written you quite boldly on some points, as if to remind you of
them again, because of the grace God gave me to be a minister of Christ
Jesus to the Gentiles with the priestly duty of proclaiming the gospel

of God, so that the Gentiles might become an offering acceptable to God, sanctified by the Holy Spirit. Therefore I glory in Christ Jesus in my service to God. I will not venture to speak of anything except what Christ has accomplished through me in leading the Gentiles to obey God by what I have said and done – by the power of signs and miracles, through the power of the Spirit. So from Jerusalem all the way around to Illyricum, I have fully proclaimed the gospel of Christ. It has always been my ambition to preach the gospel where Christ was not known, so that I would not be building on someone else's foundation (Rom 15:15–20).

This is Paul's ministry in a nutshell. He preached the gospel expecting the Gentiles not only to be saved, but to be obedient. Therefore, when Paul went out as a pioneer, he preached the gospel in the power of the Holy Spirit so that signs and wonders confirmed what he said. He then worked to make disciples of his listeners. He was, in terms of the Old Testament temple, a priestly steward of the gospel, and the Gentiles were the pleasing sacrifice presented before God.

The temple, the church, is God's dwelling place in the Spirit. Here we find his glory, offer sacrifices, proclaim the word of God and read the Scriptures. We are also stewards of the word, because Paul calls himself a priestly steward of the gospel. He goes out from the temple to reach the Gentiles with the gospel. Then he brings them into the temple as a pleasing sacrifice, sanctified and purified in the Holy Spirit. This takes place when he makes the Gentiles obedient. Paul says, in Romans 1:5, that 'we received grace and apostleship to call people from among all the Gentiles to the obedience that comes from faith'.

This means that an apostle's work, including Paul's, is never finished! When Paul preached and people believed, he then made them disciples by instructing and teaching them to obey all that Jesus had commanded. Such is the diversity of the apostolic ministry.

People must be saved, but this isn't enough. If we just preach the gospel without making the newly saved disciples, then we aren't obeying the Great Commission. In Acts, all believers were called disciples. Paul always nurtured the newly saved after completing his evangelistic and apostolic preaching. In Acts 19:8–11, we read how he set apart those who had become disciples in order to teach them daily in Tyrannus' school. He did this for two years, enabling the entire province of Asia to hear the gospel. Paul taught them, and then they went out and preached what they learned from him.

This is God's model for missionary work everywhere. If we do it this way, we'll fulfil the Great Commission.

Don't look for quick solutions

Our modern society demands instant results, and we get frustrated when we don't immediately get what we want. But in his second letter to Timothy Paul speaks of enduring hardships as a good soldier of Jesus Christ. He refers to the athlete and the hard-working farmer. The soldier, athlete and farmer work on a long-term basis.

Without a long-term perspective, you will always be frustrated. Jesus said:

> You did not choose me, but I chose you and appointed you to go and bear fruit – fruit that will last. Then the Father will give you whatever you ask in my name (Jn 15:16).

This means that when you look for the fruit of your labour two months later, it's still there. It's still there six months later and a year later, and something else has happened: the fruit has increased. This is fruit that endures. The numbers you have now aren't as important as the numbers you have tomorrow, the next day, next month, or next year!

Paul says, 'Indeed, you are our glory and joy' (1 Thes 2:20). Paul's letter of recommendation as an apostle was the visible fruit in the churches he founded. They were his pride and joy. He accomplished what he was called to do, and it produced a fruit that endured and continued to develop. You need to think this way as a minister, rather than look for quick solutions. We work more in the invisible than in the visible, more long term than short term. We will not be judged by the inspiration of the moment, but by what happened afterwards. A good tree bears good and enduring fruit.

What did Paul do to produce enduring fruit? He started churches. If you want to preserve your fruit, you must have the right environment for it. Churches must be established that will take care of the harvest, and train believers. God wants to establish and strengthen his work through local churches.

Church after church will remain in the wake of the apostle. When he looks back, he will see a work that endures and disciples who do the will of God.

Enduring fruit needs strength

Paul's ministry changed the spiritual atmosphere wherever he went. The apostolic ministry doesn't just come with a momentary surge without establishing something. Things do happen in the present, but the real effects aren't noticed until later.

Today, there is a form of irresponsibility that comes from the spirit of this world. It causes people to want to float on the surface and enjoy momentary pleasures. People lack the desire to go deeper, to take responsibility and to work with the Holy Spirit to produce lasting fruit. If these attitudes do not change, then God will hold us responsible. You cannot be nonchalant about bearing fruit. You must accept the responsibility for the people you lead to Christ, or else your fruit will never last! When you understand that it isn't about you any longer, but about people who need God, you'll make sure your fruit endures. Lasting fruit means strength. When the fruit grows stronger, the devil can't come in and tear a work apart, or knock it down.

In some situations, rebellion is total and is carefully disguised. 'I'll do as I please. I'm led by the Holy Spirit and I only do what I feel like doing.' This type of reasoning is completely wrong. You shouldn't just do what you feel like doing, but what Jesus tells you to do. 'Go into all the world and make disciples!' He didn't say, 'Go out and do that part of the Great Commission that you find enjoyable.'

God wants his order to be established, not the will of individuals. It is more important than ever to take this seriously, because God loves people. Jesus died for individuals, and he wants each of them to become a disciple.

A challenge for the entire body of Christ

Our irresponsibility towards the harvest is a collective sin of the body of Christ. We must confess the sin of not caring for the harvest, just as we have confessed other sins. We cry for revival, yet are careless with the harvest we have. Jesus wants labourers who cut the wheat, lay it on the wagon and drive it into the barn.

Imagine yourself as a farmer. You hire a man to help you with the harvest. He harvests the crop, leaves it lying in the field, and then comes to you and asks for his wages.

'I left the wheat in the field over there.'

'Oh no, it's supposed to be in the barn!'

'But there are no barns!'

'You're right. Build some, then.'

'But that's hard work. I'm not called to that!'

You are! Jesus said, 'Go out, preach the gospel, and make disciples.' If necessary, an apostle or evangelist may need to go to an area and stay there for a longer period. Paul stayed in Corinth for one and a half years, and for two years in Ephesus.

Examine your motives. They should never be money, fear, glamour or self-centredness. Instead, we should ask: 'What are the ways of the Lord? We need to follow the Great Commission the way Jesus wants, so that we'll have lasting fruit. We cannot fool ourselves and others into believing that all is well, when it isn't!'

This isn't a challenge only for evangelists, but a challenge for the entire body of Christ. Our flesh always wants to do what is quick, simple and has immediate results. Jesus wants lasting fruit. Lasting fruit in the former Soviet Union, lasting fruit in Africa, and lasting fruit in Europe. Get this into your heart! God will give you disciples who remain disciples, and become powerful in the Lord.

The war is won through endurance

Paul's ministry had depth. This is why he received so much opposition and resistance. But the enemy couldn't make his ministry transient – here today and gone tomorrow. Instead, Paul's influence continued for years, even centuries.

The enemy is afraid of constant pressure from heaven. It's far better to maintain constant pressure on the devil than to attack at lightning speed. If you continue to apply the pressure, the devil will be forced to back off eventually. No war is won by a single battle. You shouldn't be proud if you win a battle; nor should you be depressed if you lose one. You need to win more battles, and above all, you need to win the war!

In the Old Testament, one mistake was constantly repeated. The Israelites would win a battle, go home and celebrate, but forget that the Philistines were still there. The Israelites won only one battle, but God wanted them to chase the Philistines out of the country and exert constant pressure until all of Israel's territory was free.

Paul speaks about his area of responsibility in 2 Corinthians 10. He exerted intense pressure in that region until all resistance was crushed, and obedience to Christ was established.

You may be wondering: 'But this will take my whole life. Isn't this considered overtime?' That's what is necessary – your entire life. Paul says: 'I'm swamped. I work more than all of you.' He had decided not to relax until everything was done. Nothing but total victory was good enough.

Paul was constantly harassed and attacked by the enemy because he had such endurance. His ministry was always questioned:

> For some say, 'His letters are weighty and forceful, but in person he is unimpressive and his speaking amounts to nothing' (2 Cor 10:10).

This was the critics' opinion of Paul. When we read about him, we see the mighty wonders, signs and miracles he performed. The critics didn't always see these. 'There really isn't anything special about Paul,' they thought. 'Let's see some results now, Paul.

We've heard you who talk and write so much in your letters. Show us how fantastic you are!' Paul responds by saying:

> Even though I may not be an apostle to others, surely I am to you! For you are the seal of my apostleship in the Lord. . . . . Are we beginning to command ourselves again? Or do we need, like some people, letters of recommendation to you or from you? You yourselves are our letter, written on our hearts, known and read by everybody (1 Cor 9:2; 2 Cor 3:1–2).

Paul's ministry was like a plough

People always tried to point out that Paul didn't really accomplish anything special. He was constantly harassed by the devil through people's contempt, criticism and questioning. They did this because God had placed within Paul the strength to turn continents upside down. His ministry was like a plough. When a plough is at work, the largest and most important part is under the ground. It isn't visible!

Satan constantly tried to take Paul's fruit by questioning his ministry in an attempt to weaken it. He tried to push Paul aside by using other so-called apostles. 'Super apostles' Paul calls them (2 Cor 11:5). These apostles had named themselves. They didn't have Paul's power, authority, anointing, revelation or ability, nor his pervasive force either.

These so-called 'apostles' spoke for the moment. Their words sounded good, and had a certain superficial effect. They filled the theological discussion groups of the day. They had opinions and labels for everything, and were more concerned with making a name for themselves than doing the work of the Lord. These 'apostles' caused many of Paul's problems but their names were soon forgotten. Paul, on the other hand, is still remembered. He worked while others talked. If the devil had succeeded in weakening Paul's work, a few may still have been blessed, but the spiritual atmosphere wouldn't have been affected. Churches wouldn't have remained or been built, and nations wouldn't have been laid at the feet of Jesus. This was Paul's mission: to be an apostle to the nations and place them under submission to Jesus Christ.

Your reward – a work that endures

Paul's chief concern was always: 'Will there be fruit that endures?' God always comforted and strengthened him, and delivered him. The devil was furious with Paul because he personified God's ability to establish his kingdom properly. We still experience the effects of his ministry today.

Don't look to the present only, or the impact of a single meeting. God wants long-term effects, and he has promised to give fruit that endures. If your fruit hasn't yet come in full measure, it will, as you stand in faith for it and fulfil your responsibility in the harvest fields. As you meet the needs of your ministry, blessing and rewards will surely follow. John speaks of the very best reward: 'I have no greater joy than to hear that my children are walking in the truth' (3 Jn 4).